W9-BKC-468

Reconciled Sinners

Reconciled Sinners

Healing Human Brokeness

Dr. Bernard Cooke

Foreword by Doris Donnelly

TWENTY-THIRD PUBLICATIONS
Mystic, Connecticut

Twenty-Third Publications
P.O. Box 180
Mystic CT 06355
(203) 536-2611

© 1986 Bernard Cooke. All rights reserved. No part of this publication may be reproduced in any manner without prior written permission of the publisher. Write to Permissions Editor.

ISBN 0-89622-284-5
Library of Congress Catalog Card Number 86-50890

Cover photograph by Jeff Brass
Edited by Louise Pittaway
Interior design by John G. van Bemmel

Foreword

The French philosopher Paul Ricoeur once pointed out that
the Christian does not profess faith in sin but rather in the forgiveness of sin. He may not have said it loud enough. Or long
enough. For there are still far too many Christians who regard
their lives as unredeemable failures and themselves as unpardon-
able wretches. Apparently, these Christians missed the point of
the creed, the gospel, and Paul Ricoeur's fine advice to live like
the reconciled sinners they are. Instead, they opted for something
other than the new life promised by Jesus Christ.

Several things suffer as a result of a preoccupation with sin
and sinfulness: one is that *sin* is neutralized and we miss its
destructive potential to ruin us and the people we touch; *we* are
lessened because we fail to appreciate the happiness, joy, and
freedom God intended for us; and *God* is diminished because
God is imaged mostly as a tough cop or a nagging shrew eager
to pounce on us and have us pay dearly for our transgressions.

What we have needed for a long time has been a theologian
willing to tackle in a manner accessible to a wide audience the
issues and questions evoked by this lopsided approach to our
salvation. We owe Bernard Cooke our gratitude for doing just
that. Bishops and bus drivers, accountants and athletes, senators
and secretaries can all be grateful for this book.

Bernard Cooke carves out large sections of theology appropriate to this inquiry and then faces up to the persistent and tough
questions in his typically lucid and forthright way. If you are interested in knowing whether God is "angered" or "hurt" by sin,

v

or how important it is that we forgive ourselves, or how Jesus is a sacrament of God's reconciliation and how we are such sacraments, or how we humans can be so foolish as to continue doing what can only destroy us—then you have come to the right place. Dr. Cooke does not disappoint; his approach is clear, candid, and superbly balanced.

I am tempted to say that Professor Cooke has done a flawless job in these pages, but he might object to such a designation, for it is precisely his point that we are flawed (not flawless)— imperfect, sinful, irregular—but loved and forgiven all the same. And, as if that weren't enough, Dr. Cooke reminds us that it is not God's style to have us writhe uncomfortably because of our sinfulness; instead, God celebrates our return with warmth and gentleness and does not let anything we've done stand in the way of the relationship between us.

Such a gracious God will be alien to fire-and-brimstone types who thrill to a vengeful God, but Bernard Cooke's case on behalf of mercy is very convincing in spite of the opposition. So, too, is his treatment of sin which challenges us in unexpected ways about our addictions, passions, and "damned foolishness," and jolts us as individuals and as members of many communities (even the church community) to do some serious reckoning about our cowardice and hypocrisy in failing to call that which is sinful, "sin."

Without mincing words, Dr. Cooke offers some suggestions about our culpabilities and he identifies four basic divisions that need a healing touch in our own backyard: the unresolved ecumenical dialogue ("considerable goodwill still exists, but the wind seems to have gone out of the sails"); the estrangement between so-called progressives and reactionaries ("what is called for is unprejudiced trust in each other's sincerity"); the gap between the rich/powerful and the poor/powerless (a gap of "explosive alienation"); and the conflict of women in the church ("for a Christian conscience, there is no alternative. . .sexism is a sin").

When we face these divisions without pretense and evasion, the process of forgiveness and reconciliation can begin. When we face these divisions with repentant hearts, we will be authentic signs of reconciliation in a world community that can spot a phoney at a glance.

Dr. Cooke makes a bid for rituals along the way, like other processes in our lives, to signal our routing and destination before reconciliation is complete. He is quite right, I think, in broadening the events of forgiveness and reconciliation for us individually and corporately and encouraging us to find signs outside the "officially" designated ones. The truth is that we may not recognize symbols of reconciliation on the altar and in other sacraments unless these are simultaneously visible in the ordinary, day-to-day forgiving and reconciling effort of the community. That balance needs to be present for us to know ourselves as both sinful and reconciled. Bernard Cooke's term "reconciled sinners" turns out to be right on the mark in establishing our basic identity as followers of Christ.

Only a theologian as respectful of the New Testament and the tradition of the church could steer us back to our moorings with such confidence and authority. A pioneer in the theology of the sacraments for close to three decades, Bernard Cooke reminds us in this volume that when theology is also faithful to the human condition, the paradox that "less is more" pertains.

Doris Donnelly
South Bend, Indiana

Contents

Introduction

In the late eighteenth century when David Hume, one of Christianity's sharpest critics, leveled his attack against the Scottish Presbyterian religion he had experienced in his youth, he focused on the church's preaching about sin. As Hume saw it, the "fire and brimstone" sermons did little more than create anxiety and false guilt in people. Even the ancient polytheistic religions, despite their crude superstition, were not in his view as harmful to people as was modern Christianity.

Since Hume's day there have been many other voices criticizing the negative effects of religious concentration on sin. For one thing, modern psychology has provided new insights into the forces that influence human choices and human guilt. As a result, there has been a good deal of confusion about sin—some people wish to dismiss the very notion of sin as a carry-over from "medieval superstition"; others wish to return to "old-time religion" and its emphasis on human evil and the need for repentance; still others welcome the move away from over-concentration on sin but feel that sin is a reality that cannot be ignored. Many persons who should reflect more on their sin don't do so; and many good people worry more about sin than they should.

This present book is written with the conviction that the vast majority of people are basically good but not perfect, that all of us have our shortcomings and do things that harm ourselves or others. We all need to abandon some self-centered decisions and activities, to become more honest and caring and sensitive to others. But this human imperfection which we share with one another is not meant by God to be a burden of guilt that constantly weighs us down and sours our relations with one another and with God.

Instead, life should be for mature people an experience of recognizing their identity as reconciled sinners; that is, individuals who have discovered certain shortcomings, are quietly working to overcome them, are genuinely sorry for whatever hurt they have inflicted on others, and are not unduly upset with the fact that they are neither infallible nor sinless. Obviously, we are not meant to rejoice in our sinfulness; but on the other hand our sins, if we try to keep them from touching the heart of our intentions and activity, should not be a barrier to joy. Such maturity demands a more accurate understanding of Christian teaching about sin than many people have. It is my hope that at least some of these people will be helped by this book—to understand better what "sin" is, but more importantly to understand better the compassionate God who is revealed in the life, death, and resurrection of Jesus Christ.

When I behold your heavens, the work of
your fingers,
the moon and the stars which you set in place—
What is man that you should be mindful of him;
or the son of man that you should care for him?
You have made him little less than the angels,
and crowned him with glory and honor.
You have given him rule over the works of
your hands,
putting all things under his feet.

Psalm 8:3-5

CHAPTER ONE

Being Human

Our destiny is life and joy. God's action in our lives is one of liberating us from evil and freeing us for joy.

When Christian theologians in the Middle Ages wrestled with the question of sin and evil, trying to give some explanation or even a definition of evil, the best of them arrived at the insight that evil/sin is essentially a denial, an absence, of the good that should exist in a given situation. The evil of blindness is an absence of sight; the evil of sin consists in the lack of the goodness that should characterize human actions; social evils are a lack of that order and justice that should characterize human life together.

Basically the same insight was expressed centuries before in the wisdom writers' explanation of evil that is contained in the early chapters of Genesis. The story about Adam and Eve that locates the source of human suffering and death in sinful foolishness begins by describing the ideal that should be realized in life. Sin is the loss of that ideal. Eden is a situation of peace and mature happiness and enduring life. Sin destroys all this by

5

introducing death and suffering and alienation of humans from their own inner selves, from nature, from one another, and from God.

Taking a clue from these theologians of old, this book's attempt to explain today's Christian understanding of sin and reconciliation will begin with a picture of what human life can and should be; for this is what sin destroys and reconciliation at least partially restores. Any such description of "the human" must try to be both idealistic and realistic. It must take account of the limitations that are intrinsic to men and women because they are creatures living in an imperfect world, part of a history that is still far from its fulfillment; at the same time, it must avoid seeing life as essentially a series of problems and difficulties.

Meant for happiness

One of the saddest misunderstandings of their Christianity that some people have had is that the life of "good Christians" is not meant to be particularly happy—happiness is something that will come in "the hereafter" if one has persevered in virtue during this present life. Such is not the view of Jesus as it is reflected in the gospels. Although he was most aware of the suffering in people's lives and experienced keen suffering himself, he thoroughly enjoyed life. His parables indicate that he found constant enjoyment in nature around him; he enjoyed the meals he shared with people; he enjoyed the company of his close friends. At the Last Supper, as John's gospel describes it, Jesus shared in a special way the ideas and hopes that were dearest to him; and he ended by saying "All these things I have said to you, so that my joy may be in you and your joy may come to fulfillment."

This certainly does not sound like a sad approach to human life. Nor was it naive, for Jesus knew at that moment that he faced condemnation and death. Yet, there was a level of joy and happiness that nothing could negate, not even impending death. At the root of that joy was the awareness of being uniquely and unfailingly loved by the God he knew so intimately as his "Abba."

Christians are meant to share in this kind of deep joy. Their faith in being loved by God, a faith that finds confirmation in the experience of their human friendships, in loving and being loved, provides a solid sense of importance to their lives. Life is worthwhile, something in which they can rejoice, something to which they can look forward, something that has a purpose—and to which, therefore, they can give their energies and talents.

Meant for fulfillment

To achieve, to use one's talents and realize one's potential, to grow as a person is intrinsic to our humanity. One of the essential components in any situation of genuine social justice is the opportunity to develop and express our potential. People have different abilities, different interests and objectives, different contributions they can make to bettering life; but each person has the right to become what they are capable of becoming.

One of the hardest things to explain, however, is the apparent impossibility of such achievement in the lives of millions. The poverty in which they live, the lack of any educational opportunities, the total obscurity and anonymity which stand in the way of anyone helping them out of their deprived situation—all seem to negate the promise of their human personhood. Yet, we do recognize that situation as a negation, as something that should not be, as an evil. This means that we implicitly recognize that human life is meant to reach a goal, even though we can't figure out how that is to happen for much of the human race. To some extent we have no alternative but to trust in faith that God has some way of realizing this as people pass beyond death into unending life. At the same time we are beginning to realize that there rests on all of us a shared responsibility to do something about this situation, to work together for a radical change in the world's economic and social processes, so that the masses of people in deprived portions of the globe gain the opportunity for development that is their human birthright. But more of that later.

For the moment, what we are stressing is that people are meant to live as fully as possible. We are *meant for life,* life that grows and deepens here on earth, even fuller life beyond physical death. The promise that Jesus made during his public ministry was the promise of unending life. God has made us to live, to become ever more vital. God's own Spirit is, as we say in the creed at eucharist, the life-giving spirit.

Meant for freedom

Because we are meant to live as persons we are meant to be free. Freedom is an essential characteristic of personal living. To be free means that one is basically in charge of one's own life, able to determine one's own destiny. Obviously, the freedom we have is limited by the fact that we are creatures who live at a particular point in history, in a particular culture, with a particular set of experiences, etc. There are many things that I could never become, no matter how keenly I might desire them.

I might, for example, admire Thomas Aquinas or Teresa of Avila and wish that I could have been either of those personages; but that is, of course, something I am not free to do. But the essence of my freedom is that I am meant to decide who I will be, what kind of person I will become, how genuine and honest and loving and concerned I will be. I am meant to be self-determining regarding those things that are most essential to being me.

But to be free, people have to be *freed.* They have to be freed from fears that inhibit them; they have to be freed from prejudices and false information that keep them from making proper decisions; they have to be freed from the ruts in which they are stuck through years of acting unreflectively; they have to be freed from apathy and dullness; they have to be freed from a certain amount of sin that has drifted into their lives. The first step is that they need to be freed from whatever prevents them from realizing that they need to be freed; they must come to realize their relative lack of freedom, so that they can seek to be free.

Many people, perhaps most, in a country such as the United States, where political freedoms are guaranteed by law, do not know what it means to be truly free. They are not self-determining, though they could be. They seldom make their own personal decisions. They drift with the current styles, they follow the crowd, they accept the policies of their government without much questioning—as long as those policies don't interfere with their own plans and physical well-being; even basic choices about food are largely influenced by advertising and mass marketing. They equate freedom with such things as the right to vote, the right of news media to print "the truth," the right to hold and express their own opinion—rights which are important freedoms; but they do not realize the extent to which in many matters their lives are being shaped by others.

It takes several characteristics to become humanly free: courage, imagination, self-assurance, a set of values that gives priority to people rather than to things. It takes a willingness to be saved; to be liberated from the barriers to freedom, liberated by friends, by genuine learning, and by God. None of us can achieve maturity, become loving and free persons, on our own; we depend upon one another and must freely accept that dependence.

Meant for community

That leads us to the social dimension of our human existence. Everything about us, from infancy to old age, points to the fact that we are not meant to exist in isolation from one another. Even our distinctive personal identity and the autonomy that is the essence of our freedom cannot be achieved except in relationship to others.

It is more than an intertwining of needs. We are intended not only to be *with* one another but to be *for* one another. The fact that we are speaking beings makes it clear that our thoughts are not meant to be ours alone; we are meant to communicate with others, to share consciousness; to enter into other people's views, understandings, enthusiasms, and insights, and to let them enter into ours. The reality of friendship indicates that we have both the capacity and the need to care for one another, to be a support for one another, to grow together into maturity and responsibility.

Perhaps nothing speaks more clearly about this sharing of life than our human families. The experience of men and women falling in love, accepting deep personal intimacy with one another, having children—a situation of obvious and unavoidable caring on one side and dependence on the other, developing a family identity that simultaneously nurtures the emergence of distinctive personalities—all this points up the fact that community is basic to human life.

Today we have become increasingly aware of the importance of community. There are innumerable books, magazine articles, meetings, and conferences dealing with the need for community, the techniques for developing it, the barriers that prevent it, etc. The basic difficulty is that communities cannot be created artificially; real community exists when people are sharing something with one another, when in one way or another they are truly communicating; but they cannot do this unless they have something to share and really wish to share it. Communities are only as good as the people in them.

If, however, we have communities of genuine persons, human life is enriched, and people live more fully and more happily. Christianity is meant to teach and exemplify this in a special way. As the Second Vatican Council insisted, Christian communities should be "a sacrament of the world." By situations of genuine human sharing and concern and love, and therefore situations of human growth and peace and freedom and happiness, such groupings of Christians would be a sign and a promise of what the entirety of human existence could and should become.

Meant to create

The goals of human existence that we have been describing are not meant to be simply a dream. Nor are they something that we vaguely hope will come about some day because of God's saving power in our lives. They are goals that with the support of God's presence we are meant to achieve; we are meant by God to create our history, our future, in ever fuller form. Christianity has always been realistic in recognizing the obstacles that stand in the way of our reaching these goals. For one thing, the church has always taught the existence and power of sin. But Christianity has also been from its origins a religion of hope; the obstacles can be overcome. To believe that the goals can be reached is not naively idealistic.

In working for this ideal, everyone, whether Christian or not, shares a certain frailty. Failure as well as success is a part of our human experience; it is hoped that recovery from failure is also part of that experience. That is why the following chapters will attempt to clarify the root failure we call "sin" and the overcoming of that failure in "reconciliation."

To identify ourselves as *reconciled sinners,* which is what all of us are to some degree or other, need not be—indeed, should not be—a self-negating process. Instead, it should be part of the calm recognition of reality that characterizes maturity. Obviously, it involves an acceptance of salvation from God and from one another, an admission of the need for forgiveness and support from others, an honest appraisal of our strengths and weaknesses. But it is not meant, as we said earlier, to stand in the way of joy nor to block the recognition of ourselves as basically good.

Our destiny is life and joy. God's action in our lives is one of liberating us from evil and freeing us for joy.

For the man and his wife the Lord God made leather garments, with which he clothed them. Then the Lord God said: "See! The man has become like one of us, knowing what is good and what is bad! Therefore, he must not be allowed to put out his hand to take fruit from the tree of life also, and thus eat of it and live forever." The Lord God therefore banished him from the garden of Eden, to till the ground from which he had been taken. When he expelled the man, he settled him east of the garden of Eden; and he stationed the cherubim and the fiery revolving sword, to guard the way to the tree of life.

Genesis 3:21-24

CHAPTER TWO

Self-Destruction

*Perhaps a good place to begin is with a closer look
at the manner in which sin is a process of self-
destruction, destruction of the sinner as a self,
destruction of the selfhood of others. Sinful
activity is evil because of what it does to persons
as persons.*

Our world today is a world of baffling change; every aspect
of our experience is being altered by rapid development of tech-
nology, explosive increase in information, massive movements
of people from one location and one social context to another.
Even religions, which always projected the image of stability and
enduring tradition, are undergoing basic changes.

Because people have always tended to equate religion with
morality—though the two are not identical, not even inseparable—one of the most noticeable elements of this change is
the altered view today of *sin*. We can realize how deep the
challenge to traditional understandings of sin is when we hear
respectable voices asking whether there really is any such thing
as "sin."

That there are mistakes—of course; that there is deviant behavior that may threaten people—that's obvious or we would not have police and courts. But are there deliberately malicious actions that flow from men and women's moral wickedness? As we learned more about the force of psychological drives and compulsions, about the conditioning effect of economic and social deprivation, we have had to reassess the blame that we laid on people whose actions were judged to be evil. Even more basically, we have had to face the question of what we really mean by "sin."

A rather naive dismissal of sin characterized some psychological and social scientific writings of mid-century. It seems that the pendulum has now swung back from that view. As we have reflected on some of the happenings of our day, for instance the staggering evil represented by the Nazi slaughter of Jews, we have been forced to face the evil that humans bring into history. But we also have come to see that the reasons we gave for certain actions being "sinful" were far from adequate.

Sin as violation of laws

Perhaps the reason most commonly given for some act being morally wrong was that it was *a violation of law*. A sin was a deliberate refusal to follow a law that came directly from God—as presumably was the case with the ten commandments given to Moses on Sinai, or a law that came indirectly from God through legitimate authorities in the family, the church, or civil government.

It was probably inevitable that Christians should have come to think of sin as violation of laws. Christianity had taken over the Hebrew Bible as part of its own sacred scriptures; and the Bible emphasizes, from beginning to end, the law that God has given his people. New Testament writings, such as Paul's letter to the Galatians, break with this law-centered mentality, insist that Christians are freed from this Old Testament law, and describe Jesus himself as the new law. Yet, through most of the past two thousand years Christians have viewed morality as conformity to the Ten Commandments rather than as discipleship or as the assertion of Christian freedom.

Certainly, laws have an important role to play in society. They frame more clearly the responsibilities that people have to one another. They state the guarantees of security and well-being that people should have. They provide the guidelines for those in positions of authority to protect the rights of people, even of the poor and disadvantaged, against those who would exploit and injure their fellow humans.

Yet, when we go beyond laws and their external observance and look at the *morality* of Christian behavior, look at the judgment of their conscience that actions are good or evil, we find a need to say *why* some acts are good and others are bad. Laws can state that defaming another or stealing his property is unacceptable social behavior; the laws do not make these actions morally wrong. But what, then, does make certain human actions morally evil, that is, sin?

Sin as self-destruction

There are several ways that one could respond to this question, as we will try to do in subsequent chapters. But perhaps a good place to begin is with a closer look at the manner in which sin is a process of *self-destruction,* destruction of the sinner as a self, destruction of the selfhood of others. Sinful activity is evil because of what it does to persons as persons.

Let us take a clear instance of grave sin: the deliberate sexual abuse of small children by those who produce child pornography. This has recently drawn a great deal of public attention, and there is universal agreement about its immorality. In these cases we are dealing, not with emotionally disturbed individuals whose own psychological imbalance contributes in large part to their abuse of children, but with individuals who coldly and deliberately exploit little children for the purpose of making money.

It is rather clear how this callous abuse of children does great harm to the boys and girls who are the victims. Most people can only imagine the emotional trauma of a six-year-old girl, abducted on her way to school, dragged off into strange surroundings to be sexually molested and then forced into sexual acts, many of them exotic and sick, while someone is taking pictures of all this. Those who have counseled adults who had some such experience in their childhood know how deep and lasting are their psychological wounds. They find it practically impossible to think of themselves as good. Strangely, many have a sense of guilt, as if they were somehow responsible for what happened. At the same time, there is often a deep-seated anger at the world in general that such a thing could have happened to them.

In one way or another, the victims of such abuse find it almost impossible to grow into a mature person as we are meant to do. To harm someone in this way and to this extent is not a mistake; one cannot attribute it to human frailty or ignorance; it is deliberate malice—a sin.

This, of course, is a dramatic instance of a sinful action; most destruction of one's own selfhood or that of others is much less dramatic. Usually, it is a gradual nibbling away at a person's self-image, a denial of the dignity and potential of a person, an undermining of one's self-esteem and of one's hope for personal achievement and true happiness.

There are myriad ways in which we do this to ourselves and to one another. By talking about someone's faults we help destroy other people's esteem of that individual, an esteem that he or she depends upon for a positive view of themselves. When as a result of such defaming others think that I am not a good person, it is difficult to continue believing in myself as good—few of us have that much psychological security.

Or perhaps by some conniving and deceit I was able to deprive a person of the position they deserved in their profession or employment. I might have done this by cheating in a screening examination for some job, or I might have done it by reporting falsely on that person's performance in a job. In any event

I would have closed to that individual the possibilities of personal development and achievement and satisfaction that would have come with the position.

I may have rather deliberately set out to harm someone physically, or purposely taken from them the things they needed to provide for themselves and their families. And with those people I associate with every day—family and friends and co-workers—I can by my criticisms and harshness, perhaps even by abuse, slowly chip away at their optimism and serenity and positive self-image.

Self-destructive sexual sin

There is no aspect of human life in which this ability to enrich or to hurt people is more present than in what concerns our sexuality. Our sexuality is what translates our uniqueness as *bodily* persons; it is what directs us in forceful ways to deal with one another in friendship, even in intimacy. But if it enables us to love and care for and be creative toward one another, it is also a power to demean and deny and wound and pervert others and ourselves.

Obviously, actions such as rape or sexual abuse cause grave harm to another. But whenever I engage in sexual activity with another in a way that *uses* that person, when it is not an act of loving self giving to that person but rather a means of satisfying my own gratification, when it is not a commitment to the deepest kind of friendship but a way of dominating another, when it allows the other person to expect a lasting relationship that I do not truly intend, there is an insult to the dignity of that other person and subtle but very real harm to that person's self-image.

To the extent that I have been a source of harm rather than of growth to others, I have harmed myself. In failing to reverence others as individuals I have diminished myself. To be a human, a created person, means that I should *be for others.* This does not imply that I should have no concern for myself, my own happiness, my own development, my own needs.

Destructive self-centeredness

Not only is it legitimate for me to seek my own good, it is a basic responsibility. But my own true good, my most genuine achievement, my lasting happiness will come only to the extent that I am true to myself as a person; that is, that I will live in open and creative relationship with others.

If I refuse to go out to others, I am locked into my own self-centeredness. This can appear to be self-love but is really a denial of true self-love. Such refusal of love—for that is what is involved—is the very essence of sin; and one can see how radically self-destructive it is. Closed in on myself and closed off to the enrichment that comes with friendships and open dealing with people, I view life with petty narrowness, my vision of reality is distorted by my prejudices, and I grow more and more isolated and unwarmed by others' love. I am in a state of sin.

Self-destructive dishonesty

Another aspect of this state of sin is its dishonesty. As a person I am meant to love, but also to know. And as a knower I am meant to discover the reality that surrounds me. It would seem that I should have no problem in admitting that the reality which is there is really there, but this is often not the case: I see reality as I would wish it to be rather than as it actually is. At times this may come from ignorance or fear, but at other times it comes from dishonesty; an element in all sin is a more or less deliberate self-blinding.

I might, for instance, be faced with the possibility of making a great amount of money through defrauding my employer. My first reaction, of course, is a rejection of such an idea. However, as I am tempted for the third or fourth time by this possibility and again go through the process of making this decision, I can begin to rationalize, telling myself that it will not really harm him or the business, assuring myself that I have really been underpaid all these years and am only compensating for past injustice, comparing my projected fraud with what I assume is common practice in business circles, etc. In all this "reasoning" I am, obviously, being dishonest with myself. Deep down, I know that the supposed reasons I am giving are not true; but unless I can pretend that they are, I will not be able to go ahead with the fraudulent action.

If we examine the sins we have committed, we will discover this process of self-deception. What it reveals is that all sin is a going against what I am intended to be as a person. And the problem is that repeated acts of such self-blinding gradually render me incapable of seeing things truthfully. As I lose my ability to discover what is true, I lose also my ability to see the beauty that surrounds me in persons and things, because truth and beauty are interchangeable. If this self-blinding becomes deep and pervasive enough, it leads to a loss of contact with reality—which is one way of describing mental illness. There has truly been a process of destroying my selfhood.

Sin's reality as self-destruction can be seen starkly in the hardheartedness of those who callously destroy others. There is something repulsive and yet pitiable in many of the pimps who victimize women who have become involved in prostitution because of economic situations over which they have had little or no control. Scarcely less unattractive are the sweatshop operators who exploit the desperate situation of illegal immigrants for their own enrichment, or the kingpins in organized crime whose control of the drug traffic results in the destruction of uncounted human lives. Such people have really become inhuman; in them viciousness has replaced the concern for others that is the heart of true personhood.

One of the problems in assessing the reality of sin is that much of it flows not just from individual decisions and acts but from social institutions. There have always been unjust laws and unjust business or government practices—slavery, or concentration camps, or exploitative hiring of migrant workers are instances that immediately come to mind. But today we are more conscious of the extent to which large-scale economic enterprise, pervasive social attitudes and prejudices, foreign and domestic policies of powerful nations, or even the institutional aspects of religious groups can destroy the lives and personhood of millions of people.

In describing this organized, large-scale sin, our primary purpose is not to point fingers at those who exert power in business or government or church. Instead, it is to gain a more realistic and practical understanding of just where sin does exist in our world, so that we can do something about overcoming it. Instead of concentrating on blaming, the effective resolution is to work to change whatever it is that destroys people. Much of the evil in our world is systemic in character, that is, it flows from the very way in which the structures and processes of our modern world function. To eradicate the evil we must deal with it at its source. About this we will speak a bit later.

This, then, is the first way of understanding "sin": it is self-destruction. That is why it is morally wrong. Often, stating this in laws is helpful, whether civil or religious laws. But the actions in question do not become sinful because of the laws; they are sinful because in themselves, even if there were no explicit laws, they harm people.

Sin as "damned foolishness"

One of the enigmas of sin is that we do sinful things even though they do not seem to make sense. Particularly in the situation when a person quite deliberately does that which he knows from experience has brought nothing but harm and unhappiness, it is hard to see how a person can be that foolish. However, it throws a great deal of light on sin to see exactly how it is foolishness. Sin is foolishness because it does not make sense; it is quite literally "damned foolishness," since it not only leads to one's damnation but is in itself the very process of damnation. It is self-destruction.

Not everyone admits that sin is foolish: in more than one situation in our own day the successful exploiter of others, the politician or business executive who has risen to high position by cruelty and domination and bullying, the "captains of industry" who avoid public prosecution for theft only because of highly-skilled legal counsel are regarded as successful persons, even admired for their "street smarts." Those who gained less wealth or power because they believed in justice and morality are often considered to be losers; they were not wise enough to play the game in the way to win. On the surface, it is not evident that it is foolish to sin.

Biblical view of sin: Old Testament

Talking about sin as folly is not new; at least as far back as the Hebrew Bible this is a classic way of describing human evil. All ancient peoples (and for that matter, moderns as well) looked for some explanation of evil, an explanation that would help them cope with or even in some instances overcome the evils they encountered in their lives. Israel, too, wrestled for centuries with this question, especially with the source of the evils that humans brought on themselves and others.

One of the key biblical passages in which the Old Testament's distinctive insight into sin is expressed is certainly the story of "original sin"—the account of Adam and Eve in the garden. Even though the authors of this passage do not intend to describe a particular historical happening, they are describing something that is historical: the persistent sinfulness of humans that goes back as far as the human race, a sinfulness by which each human to some extent is touched and to which he or she to some extent contributes.

What the passage makes quite clear is that Adam and Eve's sin consists of being foolish, deliberately rejecting the wisdom contained in God's way and preferring the "wisdom" proposed by the serpent. What the serpent suggests is that they themselves will be able to decide what is good and evil; in that way they will be like God. But the sad fact is that they reject the true wisdom that comes from God; it is God who knows the path that truly leads to life and happiness. And the result of such foolishness?— all the evils that afflict humans in their own psychological lives, in their relations with one another, and in dealing with the world around them.

Most likely, this passage from Genesis was influenced by the "Wisdom Movement" in Israel. This is the search in which most of the earth's people at that time (around 500 B.C.) were engaged, for true wisdom that would guide them to happiness and fulfillment. Worldwide, the key problem that faced men and women was the existence of evil—such as natural disasters, but especially the evils that came from human malice, that is, from sin. Some peoples saw fate as the cause of the evils suffered; others attributed evil to devils or to gods who hated or were jealous of humans; still others believed that some people lived under a curse. The theologians of Israel, under the influence of God's revelation, placed the blame for sinful activity squarely on the shoulders of humans. Sin was not inevitable or fated; it came from people's foolish abuse of their freedom. People need not fall victim to evil if only they had the good sense to accept the wisdom offered by God, if only they followed the way of life God revealed through Moses and the prophets.

New Testament: clash of wisdoms

When we come to the New Testament there is a noticeable shift in emphasis: sin is seen as enslavement from which we are freed by Jesus's death and resurrection. But there is still the basic vision of two competing wisdoms, the wisdom of "this world" and the wisdom underlying Jesus's life and death—or to use St. Paul's language, the wisdom of the Spirit and the wisdom of the flesh. The revelation of God begun in the Old Testament continues into Christianity: those who believe that human achievement and fulfillment come from acquiring power and wealth by any means whatsoever are not truly wise.

Paul, in writing to the Corinthian Christians, admits that the wisdom of Christ does not make much sense to either Jews or Greeks; it can be accepted only in faith. If Paul were writing in our present-day world he would probably not speak of the unacceptable wisdom of Jews and Greeks; he would more likely talk about the false values of "the marketplace," the perspective of those who in the spheres of politics or business or industry exploit people, particularly the weak and the poor, to their own goals of profit and domination. Such people would judge Jesus to have lacked "street smarts"; they would look upon the gentle and those concerned to care for their fellow humans as afraid to "play hardball."

Living with uncompromising respect for what is true is still not commonly accepted as practical wisdom. The accepted "wisdom" is that one has to be sensible and bend the law a bit here and there. Today, as in the world of Jesus and Paul, faith is required if people are to follow the path of justice and concern for others. We need to *believe* that it pays to be good.

Sin as senseless

At the same time, an honest look at sin—and exploiting and diminishing people is what sin is all about—reveals that sin does not make sense. Even those who criticize and refuse Christianity, or for that matter all religion, have recognized that sin is, as we described it earlier, destructive. Obviously, it is not something desirable.

It does not make much sense to destroy myself as a person, to gradually erode my capacity to discover, to love, to enjoy people and enrich their lives, to expand my horizons by open and honest dealing with life. It makes no sense to diminish and slowly destroy my ability to be truly happy. There clearly is little wisdom in pursuing a way of life that cuts off friendships and the human warmth and comfort that comes with knowing that there are others who care for me because I am me. It certainly seems to be foolish to dull myself by sin, so that I grow insensitive to the beauty in the world and to the people who surround me.

Sin is this negative force in our lives, negating all that can bring joy and peace and excitement to our human existence. True, the prospect of these good things coming through sinful acts is part of what we call "temptation"; that is precisely why we do at times choose a path of sin. But this promise is illusory, as bitter experience has taught so many people. The very heart of wisdom is to choose life; but the aphorism of scripture is perennially true: the wages of sin is death.

That sin is basically folly, a lack of practical wisdom, has its social dimension as well. Part of the reason why so many millions of people have accepted Karl Marx's evaluation of human history is his recognition that sin in the form of exploitation of the weak does not ultimately make sense. While there is much of Marx (for instance, his denial of the God revealed in Jesus) that we would reject, there is a great deal of insight in his view that both the oppressed and the oppressor are harmed and ultimately destroyed by social injustices. Because of this injustice, society is plagued by class struggle and violence and wars. The power to make human life more enjoyable and fulfilling is squandered in foolish arms races that threaten the obliteration of the human race.

How can we humans be so foolish as to continue doing what can only destroy us? There is no rational response to that question, because sin does not make sense.

Then [Jesus] addressed this parable to them: "Who among you, if he has a hundred sheep and loses one of them, does not leave the ninety-nine in the wasteland and follow the lost one until he finds it? And when he finds it, he puts it on his shoulders in jubilation. Once arrived home, he invites friends and neighbors in and says to them, 'Rejoice with me because I have found my lost sheep.' I tell you, there will likewise be more joy in heaven over one repentant sinner than over ninety-nine righteous people who have no need to repent."

Luke 15:3-7

CHAPTER THREE

"Offense Against God"?

God does not need to be appeased, in order to become once again our friend; the gospel of John states clearly that God loved the world of sinful humans so much that God's own son was sent to restore us to life. Jesus' death is not the appeasement of divine wrath; it is God's defeat of the sin that would destroy humans.

For many of us who are a bit older, the catechetical instruction we received as children added to the notion of sin as "violation of law" the apparently more personal note that it was an "offense against God." Like so many of our religious understandings, this view of sin contains a mixture of truth and inaccuracy which we need to sort out.

It is particularly important that we examine carefully the notion of sin as "offense against God," because it colors our understanding of and relation to God, the very heart of our faith and our religious life. The danger of distorting people's faith in God and blocking the loving relationship they should have to God is very real. Unfortunately, in the course of Christian history the

27

danger involved in thinking about sin as "offense against God" has been often realized.

There is a truth that underlies the use of metaphors such as "God's anger" or "God's judgment," but we need to recognize that these are metaphors and to discover what their use, in the Bible and in Christian tradition, is meant to say to us. All too often the impression has been given that God is a stern ruler, harshly insisting on law and order, exemplifying in a preeminent way the qualities that have marked dominating, even cruel, officials in society and church. In cultural situations where legalism and policing and fear of punishment have characterized the approach to preserving social order, God has been preached as the "super police officer" who ultimately justifies and backs up earthly rulers.

We know that Jesus himself had to speak against this misuse of belief in God. If one examines his teaching, it is clear that his principal purpose was to tell people what the true God, his "Abba," was really like. The God he preached was clearly a God who demanded truth and justice and who could not countenance evil, but who did so because he loved humans and not because he was a menacing task master. Strangely, Christianity has often drifted away from this teaching of Jesus toward the view that God keeps a constant watch on human behavior, ready to punish any deviation.

Impact of patriarchal culture

Maybe it is not so strange that this drift in attitude happened, since Christianity developed in the context of a patriarchal culture. In patriarchal societies, power and authority are located in certain dominant male rulers—kings, princes, high priests. Intrinsic to their controlling role in society is their masculinity, which usually is proved by physical prowess in war or equivalent domination in other fields of endeavor. There is an unquestioned premise of men's superiority, starting out with the basic "fact" that the father is the head of the family to whom obedience is owed, even by his wife. In its better forms, a patriarchal society does not insist that men are better, but it accepts the fact that good order as established by God has placed males in positions of authority.

Because it is a common pattern for humans to legitimate the processes and institutions of their society by claiming that these came from God, that they are "divinely institutued," patriarchal cultures develop a view of God as the patriarch. God is the person who is supremely "father," the law-giving and law-enforcing head of the human family who works in history through earthly rulers who are his surrogates and who carry out what is presumed to be "the will of God." Whatever is proscribed by these earthly rulers is declared to be "sin," because it goes against the law of God. Patriarchy, with its stratification of human life into the powerful and the powerless, is viewed not as an interpretation of reality, an interpretation that might be a misinterpretation, but simply as the way things have been established by God.

But perhaps the patriarchal god is not the true God. Certainly, the prophetic tradition of Israel, while it is filled with denunciation of sin and demands for conversion and even threats of punishment, paints a much different picture of Yahweh, the God of Israel. Starting with Hosea in the eighth century B.C., Israel's god is described as a passionate and compassionate lover, a lover betrayed by adulterous Israel's infidelity. This is still the Lord of the law given to Moses; but the prophetic view of a loving God brings about a change in the law itself—a second form of the law, the tradition of Deuteronomy (which means "second law"), in which the first commandment begins "You shall *love* the Lord your God. . ." (6:5).

It may well reflect early Christianity's appreciation of Jesus' teaching about God that the gospels remember Jesus quoting the law from the book of Deuteronomy (e.g. Matthew 22:37). More than that, Jesus' parables are designed to help ordinary people know a compassionate rather than a threatening God, a God particularly interested in and supportive of the powerless, a savior and not a police officer, a God whose lordship is one of service and not of patriarchal domination. Clearly, Jesus' "Abba" is not the menacing divinity that so often has been misused by civil and church officials and by teachers and parents, misused as a "bogey man" to frighten people into submission. Obedience is a basic and cherished human attitude, but true obedience is a free response in love and not a reaction to fear.

For all too many Christians in the past, life has been a long experience of a God who constantly watched to see when they were going to commit some sin. Sin was something that seemed to be everywhere, practically unavoidable. Even if one had no clear awareness of having sinned, he or she worried that they probably had sins of which they were not conscious, or at the very least sinful attitudes and desires that vitiated their apparently good actions. People were told and actually believed that anything good in their actions came from God and that anything that came from themselves was bad.

This distorted understanding of God and of sin was particularly sad in the case of many people who genuinely loved God, whose lives were marred by the minor frailties intrinsic to human experience but who scarcely ever committed what could be called a grave sin. These people worried unnecessarily that they were in constant danger of losing God's friendship, a friendship that they cherished. Often this anxiety was erroneously encouraged as being "the fear of God," which the Bible praises as the beginning of wisdom. Fundamentally, what was wrong with this view was its implication that God was capricious in loving us, that God's attitude toward us was always in danger of changing because of our sins. Such a God bears little resemblance to the God taught by Jesus' parable about the father of the prodigal son (Luke 15:11).

Perhaps we could probe a bit further into the acceptability of categorizing sin as "offense against God" by trying to respond to two questions: 1) Is God angered by sin? and 2) Is God hurt by sin?

1. Is God angered by sin?

In our human attempt to gain some insight into the reality of the divine, a reality with which, strictly speaking, no idea or image can deal, we use metaphors. It is a bit like what we do when we try to talk about experiences such as suffering or love for which there are no genuinely appropriate words. In those instances we turn to poetry and so we do in speaking about God.

"The wrath of God" has been historically one of the most common and traditional metaphors applied to God. In some Protestant traditions even more so than in Catholicism, there is an insistence that, metaphor or no metaphor, God's anger is a reality with which we humans must deal if we wish to confront reality as it is. If human anger is a justified, indeed an appropriate, reaction of responsible people to evils they encounter, then certainly God must have some such response to the evils we humans perpetrate. It would seem almost immoral if God were indifferent to sin, if God did not become angry and in his anger punish the sinner.

What is clearly true in this intepretation of the metaphor is the incompatibility of evil with God. The goodness of God stands in radical opposition to sin; God is infinite love and the essence of sin is deliberate denial of love. The prophets who spoke for God have always demanded justice in human affairs, but justice is ultimately meaningless if there is no requital for sinfully exploiting the powerless. So, it would seem that God must rise up in rightful anger against those who would afflict and destroy "the widow and the orphan."

However, when we look carefully at the matter, there are a number of basic problems in imputing anger to God, problems that are rooted in the fact that God is transcendent, existing in a way that is utterly different from our limited human way of being. Anger is an emotion that is intrinsically tied to our bodiliness; becoming angry is a kind of change that cannot fit the constancy of divine consciousness. Anger is a response to something that happens, but God does not respond; God always initiates.

Again, the notion of God angrily punishing sins needs to be demythologized. The punishment of sin is intrinsic to the sin itself because, as we saw, sin destroys the sinner. God does not need to condemn or punish the sinner, the sinner does that to him- or herself. If I sin and am honest enough to admit it, I may well feel that I should be punished, that God should be angry with me; but that does argue that God is angry. What it does say is that I would be angry if I were God.

To put it more simply and at the same time more graphically—becoming angry does not fit God. When we stop to realize what we are talking about when we use the term "God," that is, the one who brought into existence and sustains a universe that is billions of years old, a universe whose expanding immensity staggers our imaginations, it is hard to imagine such a God being upset over my human actions that are so relatively insignificant. At the same time, if there is one characteristic of the divine that comes through clearly in the teaching of Jesus it is the immense compassion of God for our human shortcomings.

While divine existence is certainly not static, God does not change from loving us to not loving us. God is, both from the viewpoint of metaphysics and in the light of biblical revelation, utterly faithful and constant in loving, despite the human unfaithfulness in relationships with one another and with God. God does not need to be appeased in order to become once again our friend. The gospel of John states clearly that God loved the world of sinful humans so much that God's own son was sent to restore us to life. Jesus' death is not the appeasement of divine wrath; it is God's defeat of the sin that would destroy humans.

2. Is God hurt by sin?

Granted that it may not be accurate to speak of God becoming angry, does that mean that God remains completely unaffected by our human sinfulness? Isn't there some way in which God is hurt by our sins; is there not some sense in which sin is "offense against God"?

In answering this question, faith and philosophy part. Strict application of philosophical reflection would suggest that it is meaningless to talk about "hurting God," because God in the infinity that characterizes divine existence is beyond either our help or our harm. One can, of course, speak about denying to God the glory, the recognition of divine supremacy and power, that is due to him. But here, too, one is working with a metaphor, comparing God to those earthly rulers who expect others to pay some heed to their "superiority" and to respect their authority. When we examine the underlying reality of "God's glory," we realize that nothing can add to or diminish the intrinsic majesty of God. On the contrary, the glory of God—that is, the witness to divine power and goodness—is humans who by their existence and goodness are living proof of God's creative love. As St. Irenaeus said centuries ago, "The glory of God is the human person fully alive."

Jesus' teaching

So, it would seem that God can in no way be hurt by human sin. However, the teaching of Jesus, foreshadowed already in the great prophets of Israel, indicates something more. In some mysterious way, because the infinite God has freely entered into friendship with us, we can cause God sorrow and pain. Just as in a human friendship, when I have allowed myself to become involved with and concerned about another person and I freely open myself to being hurt by this friend, so God is touched by our actions, is "saddened by" or "rejoices" over what happens to us and what we become.

What other conclusion could one draw from Jesus' parable (Luke 15:11) of the father of the prodigal? In teaching this parable, Jesus was trying to tell his hearers about the God he knew in his own religious awareness, the God he knew and loved as his "Abba." Out of his own experience of feeling compassion for the people he himself had come to know, people whom he so longed to help, Jesus realized that his concern was shared with his "Abba." Jesus' own love for people and the sorrow he felt at their sinning and being sinned against was, he knew, a reflection of his Father's attitude toward these people. So, the father of the prodigal son is described as pained by his young son's insistence that he leave home and spend his inheritance, respectful of the son's freedom to determine his own path in life, grieving over what he suspects is the outcome of the son's headstrong and foolish decision. Rather than being a vengeful judge of the son's sins, the father goes out each day to watch for the prodigal's return; and when the boy does finally come back, broken but repentant, there is nothing but joy and forgiveness and relief on the father's part.

Clearly, even in Jesus' teaching of this parable we are dealing with a metaphorical approach to understanding the God who defies our descriptions, but Jesus is talking about the "Abba" whom he knows so intimately—and in that intimacy knows to be personally and compassionately concerned about us humans. When we talk this way we are, obviously, in the realm of faith. Believing in Jesus as God's supreme revelation to us, we believe that his own awareness of God, while it does not deny the insights of human reasoning about the divine, carries us beyond philosophy. And in that somewhat mysterious world of religious experience we can truly speak of God as being hurt by our sins.

God's "sorrow"

Having said that, we must still be very careful. The comparison with our human experience that seems to be valid here is that of human friendship, and perhaps the instance of human friendship and love from which we can best draw is the loving concern of parents for their children. Parents of wayward sons or daughters are hurt by their children's sins, hurt perhaps because they themselves have been harmed by these sins, but hurt most deeply because they see those whom they continue to love on a path of self-destruction. It is what the children's sins are doing to destroy the potential for goodness and a certain greatness, to destroy the prospects of real happiness, that grieves the parents.

So also, "God's sorrow" is not because God is diminished but because of the self-destruction and unhappiness that we humans bring on ourselves when we sin. We have been made for happiness; a fullness of happiness beyond our imagining is the destiny intended for us by God's creative love. John's gospel describes Jesus telling his disciples at the Last Supper that everything he had done in his teaching ministry was aimed at bringing them joy, a joy that would extend into the next life. When humans sin they reject this joy; Jesus knew that his "Abba" sorrowed when this happened.

The other side of this divine sorrow is the divine joy that occurs when a sinner turns from evil and repentantly returns to God. In what is a bit of rhetorical exaggeration, the gospel tells us that "there is more rejoicing in heaven over the return of the one that has wandered away than over the ninety-nine who did not" (Luke 15:7). This may be rhetorical exaggeration, but the point of Jesus' saying is clear: the repentant sinner is met with divine forgiveness and acceptance and not with cold recrimination. Some parents, perhaps to assert their own hurt, refuse forgiveness or at least demand redress for their suffering; they may seem to forgive but they do not forget. God, the "Abba" experienced by Jesus and cherished by Christians, is above that kind of reaction.

The response, then, to our two questions is mixed. God is not untouched by our sins; but they affect God only in that realm of mystery which God initiated by freely extending being and friendship to us humans. Because God is a lover involved in the lives of us, his beloved, we can say that it hurts God when we, his beloved, refuse to let divine love bring us to the joy intended for us. To know that this is what our sin does should lead us to regret and conversion; it should cause neither despair nor anxiety nor fear of rejection.

My friend had a vineyard
  on a fertile hillside;
He spaded it, cleared it of stones,
  and planted the choicest vines;
Within it he built a watchtower,
  and hewed out a wine press.
Then he looked for the crop of grapes,
  but what it yielded was wild grapes.

Now, inhabitants of Jerusalem and
    men of Judah,
  judge between me and my vineyard:
What more was there to do for my vineyard
  that I had not done?
Why, when I looked for the crop of grapes,
  did it bring forth wild grapes?

Now, I will let you know
  what I mean to do to my vineyard:
Take away its hedge, give it to grazing,
  break through its wall, let it be trampled!
Yes, I will make it a ruin:
  it shall not be pruned or hoed,
  but overgrown with thorns and briers;
I will command the clouds
  not to send rain upon it.
The vineyard of the Lord of hosts is
    the house of Israel
  and the men of Judah are his
    cherished plant;
He looks for judgment, but see, bloodshed!
  for justice, but hark, the outcry!

Isaiah 5:1-7

CHAPTER FOUR

Sin:

Refusing to Grow Up

There is nothing more central to being a person than friendship, loving others and being loved by them. Nor is there anything more basically creative of what we are as persons. To refuse to love is to refuse to be a person. To reject love in one's life is patently foolish, since it is to reject the source of our deepest happiness.

In his apostolic exhortation following the 1983 world synod of bishops that discussed reconciliation and sin, Pope John Paul II very noticeably stressed reconciliation rather than sin. This positive approach gives us a valuable guideline, one that accords with Jesus' own teaching, namely that we focus on restoring our link to God and of humans to one another, rather than centering our attention on what is wrong with the world.

So, the bulk of this book will try to do just that, to reflect on what reconciliation is and how it can be achieved. But because our understanding of conversion and forgiveness and penance and reconciliation is so much colored by our understanding of sin, it might be good to look briefly at four more aspects of sin before giving the remainder of our attention to reconciliation. This chapter will treat the four "faces" of sin then, as: 1) irresponsibility, 2) infidelity, 3) immaturity, and 4) alienation.

1. Sin as irresponsibility

One of the most interesting aspects of Old Testament history is the manner in which the people of Israel move over the centuries from a relatively low level of moral insensitivity to keen moral awareness. Strikingly parallel to the development of an individual human, Israel begins in a stage of punishability where the divine action is one of *training* and not yet of education. At this stage the motivation, as it is with a little child, is one of punishment or reward; one cannot yet speak of truly personal responsibility for one's behavior. Later generations of Israelites recognize this when they refer to this early period by saying "When Israel was a child. . ." (Hosea 11:1).

At this early stage of development, one cannot rightfully expect true personal human responsibility. One can disagree with their behavior, one may even have to take some action—such as punishment—to prevent or compensate for activity that is harmful, but one cannot look for children to take account of the moral impact of their actions. One does not speak of a little child as being irresponsible, though one may well have to correct a child's behavior because it is harmful to the child or to others. The child is incapable of being either responsible or irresponsible; and for that reason is incapable of sin.

It may sound strange to say it, but to some extent it is true that a person must be grown up before he or she is capable of sinning. The purpose of becoming an adult is not, of course, to be able to sin; it is to be able to face life with deliberate determination of one's actions, to be able to face the responsibility of caring for oneself and others. But with the possibility of being responsible comes the possibility of neglecting or refusing to live in that way.

That is not to say that the responsible and irresponsible are equally adult. When we say of a young person, "He's just having his fling before he settles down," we are in effect saying that despite chronological adulthood that person has not yet reached personal maturity. But more of the relation between sin and immaturity in a moment. For now, we can take a closer look at the link between irresponsibility and sin.

Why be responsible?

On the surface, it does not seem morally wrong to be irresponsible as long as this does not involve deliberately harming someone else. One could say—and many do—"After all, my life is my own and I have a right to do or not do what I choose." Or as the popular song has it, "I did it my way."

However, to approach life this way is to ignore the fact that to be a person means to be for others in order to become myself. It is true that I am free to make my life what I will, but that does not mean that I will be right and wise in refusing to become what I should be. Not that I must live with a heavy burden of feeling obligations all the time; on the contrary, a sense of humor and a certain light-heartedness are essential if one strives over the long haul to make the most out of life.

Without using precisely that language, Christian catechesis has traditionally taught that irresponsibility is sinful. The language that was used was "sins of omission"—a term that was so vague and general that it had little practical meaning for many people. On the lists of sins that were given people to help them examine their conscience before going to confession there was explicit mention of "sins of commission"—telling lies, stealing, losing one's temper, etc.—and then some short general mention of sins of omission.

Some cases of omission were rather clear. Jesus' parable about the man helped by the Samaritan (Luke 10:30) described such a situation. Before the Samaritan came along to care for the poor man who lay by the side of the road after being robbed and beaten, two other "responsible citizens," a priest and a Levite, had passed by without helping. It is clear from the parable that Jesus sees the behavior of these two as reprehensible. When a parallel instance occurs today, when people on a city street or in a housing complex do not help a man being mugged or a woman being assaulted because they "do not wish to get in-volved," we know that something is deeply wrong with such refusal to help another.

Self-centered unconcern

Such instances illustrate the point, but they are exceptional. For the most part there is not a clear-cut lack of action that we can identify as a "sin of omission." Instead, there is a basic attti-tude of unconcern, of self-centeredness, of not wishing to be bothered, of seeking only one's own comfort and pleasure and diversion, that makes a person dull to caring for others. He or she simply does not see the needs of others, because deep down they do not wish to bother. For the most part, there are not sins of omission but a pervading sin of omission, an enduring state of irresponsibility.

Reflection on the sinfulness of such irresponsibility indicates that this aspect of sin is increasingly significant in our present-day world. Because of the complexity of life and the prominence of large-scale organizations, much of our activity today is cor-porate; we act as elements in huge, almost impersonal, under-takings. In such contexts, where it is not always clear who is responsible for the decisions that guide the activity, it is all too easy to avoid any questions about the morality of the action, to lose oneself in the corporate crowd, to accept the decisions of "those at the top" and so avoid conflict. But is it not sinful to leave unchallenged those policies of our government that sup-port the murder of innocent civilians in third-world countries? Is it moral to share in scientific research whose only purpose is to develop weapons capable of obliterating the human race? Can we earn our living by working for a multinational company that we know is engaged in exploiting workers in this country and abroad? These are not easy questions to answer. Far from it, because there often seem to be no practical alternatives. But they are the questions we must face together if we pretend to live morally. Responsible participation in human life today, implementing the gospel precept of caring for one's brothers and sisters, will probably involve more and more shared attempts to be moral, more and more shared challenges to the systemic evil that is harming millions of people. Just as much of our sinning today is corporate, so also our "avoidance of sin" will have to be a shared undertaking.

2. Sin as infidelity

We spoke earlier about the way in which the people of Israel in the early period of their history were in a pre-sinning stage, certain actions were seen as forbidden and punishable, but there was not yet what could be truly called "personal culpability." This deeper insight of moral responsibility came with the great Israelitic prophets. In their teaching, beginning with Hosea in the eighth century B.C., the principal image of the relationship between Yahweh and the people is that of husband and wife, and the sinfulness of Israel is characterized as adultery.

To make the comparison more vivid, Yahweh apparently told the prophet Hosea to seek out and take back his wife who had left him, perhaps to become a temple prostitute in a pagan shrine, so that this could be a symbol of Yahweh's relationship with the people Israel.

"Go again and love a woman loved by another man, an adulteress, and love her as I, the Lord, love the Israelites although they resort to other gods and love the raisin-cakes offered to their idols" (Hosea 3:1).

The prophetic accusation that Israel is an adulterous people is not an accusation of specifically sexual misdeeds; rather, it is blaming the people more generally for being unfaithful to the God who chose them in love to be his favored people.

It was only when the people of Israel began to understand their relation to God in more personal terms, when the notion of loving God began to replace the idea of having to stay on the good side of a powerful divine being, that the understanding of sin as a betrayal of persons could take shape. And it is at this point that one can more properly speak of "sin." It is when one is aware of what it means to love and be loved, and aware of the implications of personal relations as being unique and ultimate, that one can start to appreciate the evil involved in denying and betraying love.

There is nothing more central to being a person than friendship, loving others and being loved by them. Nor is there anything more basically creative of what we are as persons. To refuse to love is to refuse to be a person. To reject love in one's life is patently foolish, since it is to reject the source of our deepest happiness.

Commitment to continued love

Yet, it is part of the enigma of sin that in greater or lesser ways we are unfaithful to our friends, or to those others who are not our close friends we do not even give the basic care and concern we owe to any fellow human being. Whenever we sin, we refuse in one form or another to give the love which the situation demands of us. Even in sinful actions that seem to touch no one but ourselves there is a fundamental refusal to love ourselves.

Speaking of sin as infidelity leads us to see that often there is no clear line between actions that are sinful and those that are not. We humans must learn to love, learn what is appropriate not just to friendship in general but to each particular friendship, learn what is involved in reverencing the personhood of all the persons who enter into our life experience. This learning is dependent upon our willingness to relate to others honestly, our willingness to somewhat limit our quest for personal gain or power in order to be part of a community of people, our willingness to commit ourselves to caring for others. The worth of such commitment is being questioned today as never before. We are still under the influence of the excessive stress on individuality that has characterized modern times; we are not yet sufficiently open to the value and need of human community. At the same time, the extension of our lifespan makes fidelity to friendships a much longer promise. Increased awareness of the stages of development through which each of us passes in our lifetime makes many wonder if we can commit ourselves to what we will be ten or twenty years from now.

All this does not mean that fidelity is impossible. It means, though, that it involves decisions; it does not just happen. It means that a controlling decision to be true—to myself and to others—is the root of genuine morality. Sin is a lack of or a violation of such a decision.

3. Sin as immaturity

The ability to love authentically and to act responsibly are universally recognized as the hallmarks of human maturity. Conversely, persons are judged to be immature if they are incapable of friendship and care and act without considering the consequences of their actions. But if, as we have just seen, sin is irresponsible and a betrayal of love, sin must be characterized as immature behavior.

Logical as that conclusion is, it faces a severe challenge from people's ordinary judgments. It is precisely people who sin gravely and consistently whom we see to be in some respects most "adult" because they most lack the innocence and naivete we associate with childhood. Some of the contexts in which we use the term "adult," such as "adult films," reflects this view that people who pursue a life of deliberate evil are truly grown up. Another reflection of this view is found in many of the novels and movies that glorify the lawless gunmen of "the wild West," or for that matter in the current depiction of "adult" behavior in television's soap operas.

Unjust use of power

A more important challenge to the judgment that sin is immature behavior comes when we look at the sins of exploitation and injustice committed by people of wealth and power. Even if we strongly disagree with activity that harms poor and helpless people, we do not think of it as immature. Ruthlessness, exploitation, and injustice create a false image of strength because they depend upon physical power. Bullies look strong. But the look is deceptive; the strength involved is not that which characterizes adults who have enough personal poise and self-possession to deal with other people as equals. Gentleness and caring require personal strength.

In our more negative moments we speak of public life, of business and industry and professional involvements, as "a jungle." No doubt we are using the term loosely, but it does indicate that we see much of what goes on as somewhat less than truly human, as ruled by raw expediency and not by consideration for others. But because we have elevated achievement of wealth or power to the level of unchallenged goods that justify whatever means are required to obtain them, we do not characterize unjust behavior in this sphere as either sinful or immature.

Probably the reason why we so seldom look upon ruthless use of power and wealth as immature is that our values have been little touched by the teaching of Jesus of Nazareth. We love the sound of the Sermon on the Mount where Jesus talks about God's care for the birds of the air and the flowers of the field (Matthew 6:26); but we find little practical common sense in his exhortation to care first for the things of the spirit and to spend less energy worrying about material gain (Matthew 6:25). Like Adam and Eve in the garden we do not see the guidance given by God as truly wise; we do not see those who reject this divinely-given wisdom as immature and foolish.

But Jesus' teaching also gives the criterion for judging actions as wise: look at the results. A good tree bears good fruit. And the story of Adam and Eve describes the results of sin; it does not fulfill the promise of making us like gods; it does not bring joy and peace and human community; instead it causes alienation at every level of human existence.

4. Sin as alienation

Describing sin as "alienation" brings us about as close as we can come to an insight into the intrinsic evil of sin. Sin is of its very essence a destructive force, destructive because it splits apart rather than unifies. Unity is required for societies to exist, for life to continue, for us to have psychological health and happiness; to destroy unity is to destroy community and life and personhood.

When one approaches the study of sin as alienation, one is faced with the whole of biblical theology; because "alienation" and its opposite, "reconciliation," are probably the most basic categories most commonly used by today's sociologists in describing the tensions within human society.

Rather than develop in any detail the topic of sin as alienation it should be sufficient to suggest briefly how sin causes disunity in a person's psychological existence, in human society, even in the physical world that is our environment. The theological base for such suggestions is given by the passage in Genesis to which we already referred, the short section that tells the story of Adam and Eve's sin, a sin that resulted in their being alienated from God, alienated in their own consciousness from the psychological integrity they had previously enjoyed, alienated from the earth from which they must now wrest their existence, alienated from the animal world about them, and alienated from one another as Cain kills his brother.

Separated from self and one another

On the individual level, sin keeps us from being the self we are intended to be—it alienates us from our true selfhood. Because it always involves an element of self-blinding, sin does not allow us the open and honest acceptance of reality that is basic to mental health. Because it involves a refusal to go out to others in caring concern, sin blocks attainment of the power to love that is essential to mature selfhood. As modern existentialist philosophy has rightly stressed, to exist as truly human we must live authentically; but because it is a denial of such authenticity, sin alienates us from our true humanity.

It is quite obvious that sinful actions separate us from one another. Friendships are broken, families are split apart, working partnerships become impossible, people physically injure each other—because of infidelities, injustices, dishonesty, or self-centeredness. Rivalries and hostile aggressiveness turn us into enemies of one another, isolate us from one another.

And on the larger scale, human society is often marked by tensions and oppositions rather than by community. One need not be a Marxist to notice the tension between classes in our society, tensions between rich and poor, between powerful and powerless, between racial groups, between women and men, tensions that are rooted in pervasive and long-standing injustices. One need not be "a prophet of doom" to realize that we are far from the loving concern for one another, far even from honest justice towards one another, that would root a situation of societal peace. The dangerous symptom of the radical alienations in our society is the drift towards global nuclear war, a drift we cannot seem to reverse because we lack sufficient trust in one another.

Fortunately, however, the story need not end with our sinfulness. The possibility of our becoming faithfully related to one another, of becoming honest and realistic in dealing with life, of becoming maturely responsible for ourselves and others, of living by divine wisdom, does exist because of God's saving presence in our midst. The alienations that threaten us can be overcome, because we have a savior God who has brought reconciliation through the death and resurrection of Jesus. It is to this reconciliation that we can now turn our attention.

Yes, God so loved the world
that he gave his only Son,
that whoever believes in him may not die
but may have eternal life.
God did not send the Son into the world
to condemn the world,
but that the world might be saved
  through him.
Whoever believes in him avoids
    condemnation,
but whoever does not believe is
    already condemned
for not believing in the name of God's
    only Son.
The judgment of condemnation is this:
the light came into the world,
but men loved darkness rather than light
because their deeds were wicked.
Everyone who practices evil
hates the light;
he does not come near it
for fear his deeds will be exposed.
But he who acts in truth
comes into the light,
to make clear
that his deeds are done in God.

John 3:16-21

CHAPTER FIVE

Forgiving Self

Conversion is a process; it does not happen in an instant, just as sin does not. That means that we must learn to be patient with ourselves, not weakly and irresponsibly excusing our failings but also not becoming discouraged because we have not achieved moral perfection.

Most Christians have been raised with the understanding that forgiving sins is something that God does, often through the agency of the church in the confessional. We have been told, too, that we must forgive other people's sins against us. So it may sound strange to say that we must learn to forgive ourselves, that the basis for all forgiveness of sin is a person's reconciliation with himself or herself. Actually, however, this is just another way of expressing the truth that authentic love of oneself is the base for all love of others. Once we see more fully what is involved in being reconciled to oneself, the radical importance of self-forgiveness should be more evident.

Admission of guilt

The first element that enters into reconciliation with oneself is the frank admission that such reconciliation is necessary. That is to say, one must admit that one is a sinner, that at least some of one's attitudes and actions are basically immoral and un-Christian, and that in a fundamental way one is betraying the potential to be a person and a disciple of the risen Jesus.

Such an admission, of course, is not easy; but without it there can be no turning away from sin and no reconciliation. When we are in situations of sin, our tendency seems to be one of trying to rationalize away the evil involved. We try to pretend that there really is little or no harm being done, that the matter is really of minor importance, that one has to be careful not to become too scrupulous, and so on. We cannot, however, start to turn away from a state of sin unless we admit to where we now are.

Suppose (continuing an example we used earlier) that I have been constantly defrauding my employer, carrying on what seems to be a foolproof process of gradually extracting money through minor computer manipulation. I justify the action by telling myself that there is no harm to the company, that much more money is wasted on foolish company expenditures, that I am worth more to the company than I am being paid, etc. Deep down, I have a lurking suspicion that I am not really being honest with myself; but I manage quite successfully to ignore this unwelcome insight.

Quite clearly, there is no hope that I will alter this pattern, that I will get out of a deliberately chosen situation of evil-doing, unless I admit that it is evil-doing. There is no hope that I will come to forgive myself for being a dishonest cheat, forgive myself for betraying the trust that had been placed in me, unless I recognize honestly that I am cheating and betraying a trust.

The need to admit sin is rather clear in such an instance. Often, however, the issue is not that evident; the evil involved is so engrained in a person's attitudes, or in the attitudes of the culture in which he or she lives, that it is extremely difficult to identify it as sin. Take for example the grave injustices connected with racial prejudice in our country. Until the civil rights movement drew our attention to it more than two decades ago, most of us whites were unaware of the deep sinfulness of our cultural attitudes toward our black sisters and brothers. We could not earlier have repented of these attitudes, tried to change them, and begun to make some restitution, because we were not aware of the sin. Even now, we find it hard to acknowledge the extent of economic and social injustice suffered by our black fellow citizens, injustice for which we share responsibility.

Recognition of our corporate guilt does not mean that as individuals we should accuse ourselves unrealistically of sin. We have not been responsible for creating the original unjust situation; we are not guilty of that; we do not need forgiveness for that from ourselves or anyone else. But we are involved in continuing the injustice unless we are working to correct it. We are guilty if we do not work with others in eliminating prejudice and its results from our society. Above all, we are guilty if we do not work to eradicate prejudice from our own attitudes.

But the point here is not to sort out the nature and extent of the responsibility that we share for sins that permeate our culture. We will try to do that in a later chapter. For now, what I want to indicate is the obvious fact that we cannot begin to turn away from our sins and forgive ourselves for them until we admit that they are sins.

Conversion

The second step, already partially achieved by honest admission that we have sinned, is that of *conversion*. We must decide, not just in principle but practically in a given situation, to change our attitude and behavior. What is required here is rather clear when there is a question of a specific immoral action, such as some fraudulent business practice. It is less clear when the needed conversion has to do with basic attitudes, such as prejudices or self-centeredness or dishonesty. In such cases it is obvious that conversion, a genuine *metanoia*—which means "a change of mind"—can occur only gradually. The conversion needed for true self-forgiveness is the decision to undertake this gradual shift in outlook.

Several things need to be said about moral conversion. The first is that effective conversion is always *to* something and not simply *away* from something. We only choose to do something or become something because we see it as good. Whatever the previous sin was, we had chosen it, at least implicitly, because we had convinced ourselves that it was good. During the process of conversion we had come to discover that it was not a true good, that in sinning we had deceived ourselves. But we will not fully turn away from the attraction of that apparent good, we will not persevere in the process of conversion, unless there is something else more attractive that motivates us. The key, then, is to concentrate on the goal we have in mind, what it is that we wish to gain, rather than on the sin we have decided to abandon.

Second, conversion is a process; it does not happen in an instant, just as sin does not. When we are involved with the basic options that deal with good or evil—whether we will be honest or deceitful, whether we will be concerned about or exploitative of others—conversion is a lifelong process. That means that we must learn to be patient with ourselves, not weakly and irresponsibly excusing our failings but also not becoming discouraged because we have not achieved moral perfection.

Third, both Old and New Testament scriptures make it clear that true conversion comes about as a response to the word of God. Jesus, like the Israelitic prophets before him, taught so that people would be converted to the kingdom of God, that is, to allow God's truth and love to govern their lives. What that says to us is that it is important to expose ourselves to hearing that word—as it comes in scripture, in liturgical celebrations, in the teaching of the church, in the lives of our fellow Christians. And having then encountered God's word as it is addressed to us, we must listen without twisting its meaning to meet our own desires.

So fundamental is this openness to God's word that one of this century's greatest theologians, Karl Rahner, claimed that the essence of being truly human was to be "hearers of the word."

Forgiving ourselves

Having admitted our sinfulness and turned from it in conversion, we must then go on to forgive ourselves—which often is much more difficult than one would suppose. Our self-image may have been unrealistically inflated, and we find it almost impossible to forgive ourselves for having betrayed the ideal we thought we were living. How could *we* have done such a thing, been so unfaithful, failed to live up to what we wanted to be and thought we were? We just cannot understand how we became a sinner—which is not too surprising, since sin is essentially un-intelligible.

At this point a person can become discouraged, can become obsessive about his or her moral failure, can forget the basic goodness still possessed. The person should recognize this fundamental goodness, should admit that he or she is still searching to achieve the ideals always espoused, should see that occasional moral failure is common to the human situation, and should accept the situation as a challenge to conversion rather than a cause for despair.

At such times all of us could learn from the children's TV program "Mr. Rogers' Neighborhood." While there are many good features about this program, one of the healthiest elements in it is the song "Even good people sometimes do bad things." Obviously, the song is not intended to excuse children's mischief or selfishness carelessly, but it does indicate to children that they should not allow wrong behavior to suggest the notion that they are bad persons. Genuine, straightforward recognition that we have sinned, if we have, is healthy and an element in achieving moral adulthood; brooding over our misdeeds and refusing to forgive ourselves for being less than perfect prevents us from going ahead with life and concentrating on doing things that are positive and creative. There is a profound truth in the adage that "the perfect is the enemy of the good."

Such willingness to forgive oneself, not to settle for mediocrity or to abandon one's ideals but to admit one's humanity, is inseparable from the development of a realistic self-image. And the gradual emergence in one's consciousness of a self-image that is honest and corresponds with "reality" is the process of growing into maturity. All of us need to learn gradually what the "real me" is, to assess frankly and gratefully the assets and the limitations we possess, and to recognize that this "real me" is unique and of inestimable worth.

God's forgiveness

Here, of course, Christianity's message of the salvation that has come through Jesus as the Christ proves to be the key to reconciling our personal greatness and our moral frailty. The ultimate ground for our being able to claim dignity and worth as a person is the fact, which we accept in faith, that each of us is personally loved by the infinite God. Even on the human level, being loved by others makes it possible for us to recognize that we are lovable, that is, good. Being the object of God's love, being linked in friendship with the Transcendent, provides one with an unshakable trust in one's goodness, even in the face of sin.

God as revealed by Jesus is intent on forgiving sinners. Jesus himself told his auditors that he had come, sent by his Father, precisely for those who needed healing, for sinners (Matthew 9:13). Time after time Jesus made this point in his parables—the shepherd who goes out to seek the lost sheep (Luke 15:4), the father of the prodigal son (Luke 15:11), the king who forgives the debts of his subjects. As we saw, there is no need to appease this God because of our sins; God's forgiveness anticipates our recognition of our sin, our conversion, and our self-forgiveness—actually, it makes those possible. John's gospel describes Jesus teaching—in advance even of his reconciling of life and death—that God so loved the world of sinful humans that he sent Jesus, his own Word and Son, so that humans could be saved from their sin.

But the link between God's forgiveness and our self-forgiveness goes even deeper. The latter is, in the fullest sense, a sacrament of the former. Our forgiveness of ourselves bespeaks the divine forgiveness, lets us know that we are forgiven by God, precisely because the divine forgiveness is present within our self-forgiveness, making it possible. What this says in terms of sacramental theology is that the very heart of the Christian sacrament of reconciliation is a Christian sinner's decision to forgive her- or himself. This is what we are meant to recognize and to celebrate in our liturgies of reconciliation.

Do we need God's forgiveness?

In speaking about the need for us to forgive our own sin, and the basic effectiveness of such self-forgiveness, we might logically begin to wonder just what happens to the traditional notion that we must be forgiven by God. And that wonder is good; because most of us need to deepen, even correct somewhat, our understanding of what we mean when we say that "God forgives our sins." First of all, it is true that we need to be forgiven by God and that God does forgive us. But having said that, we need to ask what is really involved.

The true God, the infinite creative power revealed to us as "personal" in Jesus' experience of this God as his "Abba," is absolutely faithful and unswerving in a compassionate love of us humans. God does not go from being displeased with us to being once more friendly; God, as we saw earlier, is infinitely above being offended and does not ask to be appeased. God's forgiveness is not a response to our admission of guilt and our conversion; it is their cause.

In some ways a loving parent's way of dealing with a child gives us an insight into the divine attitude towards human sin: while the parent will lead the young person to recognition of misdeeds and at a certain age to a sense of culpability, while the parent will work to help the child change to a better attitude and a better pattern of behavior, the parent's forgiveness of the child does not wait for some appeal for that forgiveness. Instead, the forgiveness is assumed even before the child's "sin." It is never retracted at any point and is a personal force that energizes the parent's efforts to lead the child toward moral responsibility.

God's creative love

Actually, what is at work here in God's forgiveness of our sin is God's creative power opposing the force of evil. God's act of creating is identical with his self-gift to us. There are not two divine actions, one by which the physical universe is progressively brought into being and sustained in its existence and another by which God relates to us in personal care and friendship. Rather, there is one integrated activity of creative loving which finds its focus and culmination in that concern for humans which we call "salvation."

The radical evil, sin, and the evils that flow from it are rooted in human refusal to love. Even though humans are the source of this evil, it has a mysterious force that humans by themselves are powerless to overcome. Having renounced love, it seems that we are not able by ourselves to regain the ability to ground our lives in love and concern. What is needed is the entry into human history of a love greater than our own, a love powerful enough to destroy the death-dealing power of sin. The only life-force sufficiently powerful to overcome death and sin is divine loving, personified in the Spirit of the risen Christ and his "Abba." Another way of saying the same thing is to say that we humans need to be saved by God.

Accepting salvation

However, because the process of salvation is one of love causing life, it cannot work without the free cooperation of the humans who are being saved. As we saw earlier, we need to be healed from the damage our sin does to us, but we must heal ourselves. Healing is something a living being must do—outside agents can aid, can supply things like medicine that are needed to make the healing possible—but the healing has to take place within the sick or injured being. This is true physically; it is also true psychologically.

This means that we must be willing to be saved; we must be willing to acknowledge our need for God's healing love; we must admit our dependence. This is where the rub comes, where accepting salvation from God cannot come without the sincere conversion we already described. When we sin—and we are talking about deliberate sin and not the frequent and lesser failings that we all have to work against—we refuse to accept dependence, we want to run our own lives no matter what anyone else says, including God. But to accept love from someone, and above all the love coming from God that demands a total response, we must admit dependence.

This is not a demeaning kind of dependence. In fact, as we give ourselves to a friendship we discover that the mutual dependence of the relationship gives dignity to both persons and its own kind of deep independence. So, being willing to admit our need for God's saving love and to accept it gratefully has a positive rather than a negative effect on our self-esteem. As we allow the sense of being loved by God to permeate our consciousness, we heal psychologically from the anxieties and hostilities and callousness and dishonesty that accompany sin.

So, while it is essential that we forgive ourselves for our sin, this can only happen within the context of our being freed by the presence of God's love in our lives. This is what we celebrate in our liturgies of reconciliation, particularly in the eucharist.

The scribes and the Pharisees led a woman forward who had been caught in adultery. They made her stand in front of everyone. "Teacher," they said to him, "this woman has been caught in the act of adultery. In the law, Moses ordered such women to be stoned. What do you have to say about the case?" (They were posing this question to trap him, so that they could have something to accuse him of.) Jesus bent down and started tracing on the ground with his finger. When they persisted in their questioning, he straightened up and said to them, "Let the man among you who has no sin be the first to cast a stone at her." A second time he bent down and wrote on the ground. Then the audience drifted away one by one, beginning with the elders. This left him alone with the woman, who continued to stand there before him. Jesus finally straightened up and said to her, "Woman, where did they all disappear to? Has no one condemned you?" "No one, sir," she answered. Jesus said, "Nor do I condemn you. You may go. But from now on, avoid this sin."

John 8:3-11

CHAPTER SIX

Jesus: Sacrament of God's Reconciliation

Whatever Jesus does is grounded in his concern for and love of people. But precisely because he does love the men and women and children he meets, he cannot bear to leave them in their sin, leave them alienated from his Father.

When we talk about sin or about God's forgiveness we are faced with two mysteries; but they are two utterly different kinds of mystery. Sin is a mystery in the sense that it is unintelligible, that it can find no reasonable explanation nor positive definition. Sin is unreasonable foolishness, as explained earlier. God's forgiveness, on the other hand, is a mystery because we cannot grasp why the transcendent God should be concerned about us humans.

That the infinite being we call "God" should have any personal concern for us is difficult enough to accept. That God should reach out to us in our sin to save us from the destruction we try to bring upon ourselves is more than difficult to believe. Yet, one of the fascinating things about a study of the great world religions is that there seems to be some underlying sense that "the ultimate," no matter how one thinks of it, is *compassionate.* In Christianity the belief in a saving and forgiving God is grounded in the life, death and resurrection of Jesus of Nazareth.

Jesus as savior

For many Christians this link of divine forgiveness with Jesus has been misunderstood in a way that really destroyed the notion of God as compassionate. According to this faulty view God had been angered by human sinfulness, had closed to them the possibility of final salvation and happiness, and had justly condemned the entire race to eternal perdition. Fortunately, however, Jesus by his suffering and death had appeased the divine wrath, had satisfied divine justice, and had once again won salvation for his human sisters and brothers.

Now it is certainly basic to Christian belief to see Jesus as savior from sin. But, as we saw in an earlier chapter, it runs contrary to the teaching of the New Testament writings to view the Father of Our Lord Jesus Christ as someone who requires appeasement. God desires and initiates the salvation of sinful humans. Jesus is savior because he carries out in his life and death and resurrection the saving work that his Father is doing in and through him. Because Jesus' saving activity flows from his Father's Spirit working in him, that activity is a revelation of the divine forgiveness. Jesus, as some scholars today are saying, is a parable of the divine saving presence in human life; everything he was and did told the story of God's saving presence in our human history.

St. Paul, as he reflects upon the salvation that has come through Jesus' death and resurrection, looks upon that saving activity as a multiform reconciliation, a reversal of the many alienations and hostilities that separate humans from one another and from God. Since "alienation" is the most common model according to which human sin is viewed in the Bible, it is clear that Paul's perspective is one in which the divine action in Jesus is a reversal, an overcoming, of sin. Jesus' death and resurrection are the final victory of God over the death-dealing power of evil. In studying Jesus' struggle against sin we can then most deeply probe the notion of "forgiveness of sin," for that struggle was carried on by a human who embodied (and still embodies) what God is saying to us; Jesus is God's Word incarnated.

Jesus' life as reconciliation

So, what do we learn when we turn to Jesus' life? First of all, there is a profound and unbroken sympathy with humans in their sufferings, their weaknesses, even their malice. As the gospel narratives make clear, Jesus does not take a weak or an "it really doesn't matter" attitude toward sin. Just the opposite; he is profoundly bothered by what sin is doing to people. But he is always open to and understanding of the sinner, eager to lead him or her to a different way of life, ready to aid the person in the struggle to break sin's enslavement. Time after time, when sinners came or were brought to him—the woman who washed his feet with her tears in the house of Simon, Zacchaeus the publican who climbed the sycamore tree to get a glimpse of Jesus, the woman taken in adultery—Jesus dealt with them gently.

It was not just that Jesus could speak for God in forgiving these persons their sins; it was the way he did it. As one reads the pages of the gospels one never gets the impression that sinners felt cowed in Jesus' presence, that he projects any kind of "holier than thou" attitude. Rather, he shows great respect for the personal dignity of all people. And while he speaks out forcefully against sin and as in Israel's prophets before him exhorts his hearers to recognize and abandon their sins, there is never an occasion on which he tries to intensify the repentant person's sense of guilt.

When we put this together with the often-repeated statement of the gospels that Jesus in his public ministry to people had the constant realization that he was acting as his "Abba" wished him to act, that he was guided and animated by his "Abba's" own Spirit, it is clear that the God who works through Jesus is—to put it into human terms—deeply sympathetic with people in their needs and desirous that they be freed from the influences that would diminish their personhood. God is not interested in people groveling before the divine power, declaring how evil and unworthy and worthless they are. God is interested in people honestly admitting the sin that has marred their life, for this is necessary if they are to turn to a more truly human way of being.

There is a marvelous passage in Paddy Chayevsky's play *Gideon* which, if not that theologically sophisticated in its depiction of the divine, does catch the spirit of the biblical insight into God's dealings with humans. Gideon, one of the "judges" raised up by God during the period between the exodus from Egypt and the establishment of the Davidic kingdom, was according to the short narrative in the Bible neither a paragon of virtue nor a natural leader. So, in his play Chayevsky has Gideon turn to God and declare his ineptitude, his unsuitability for the role thrust on him. But instead of agreeing that Gideon's human frailties are a reason for picking someone else, God tells Gideon that it is precisely humans of flesh and blood, women and men who do make mistakes and even sin, that God wishes to have as instruments for the divine saving action.

Jesus' call to conversion

So, too, whatever Jesus does in his dealings with those in sin is grounded in his concern for and love of people. But precisely because he does love the men and women and children he meets, he cannot bear to leave them in their sin, leave them alienated from his Father. Even if it means that he must speak out in condemnation, as he did with calloused religious officials who were exploiting the common people, Jesus demands that his hearers convert, truly convert. He minces no words, for he is acutely aware that there is no alternative: unless a person is willing to break with the sin that is the root of death, it is impossible for that person to be brought to the unending life that is the destiny intended by God.

However, there is something most instructive about the way Jesus, the eschatological prophet, calls his contemporaries to conversion. He does so by telling them about his "Abba," about the God he knows in his own uniquely intimate awareness of the divine. If people cling to their sins, it is because they believe that there is some good that will come to them—pleasure, companionship, power, or whatever it may be. Some other greater good must be promised them, a good that can outweigh the good attached to their sin—and Jesus proposes his Father as that good. Possession of God as one's friend is "the pearl of great price" for which a person would gladly give up everything else if that were necessary.

Jesus does point out, in no uncertain terms, that "the wages of sin is death"; for sin is the rejection of life. Fear of punishment is a motivation that brings many people to the point where love of God can become an effective force in their conversion—and Jesus, as a skillful teacher who deals with people the way they are, never neglects to emphasize the ultimate evil that will come with sin. But even the threat of final loss will not move people if they do not understand what it is that they will lose. If they do not know about the God who wishes to bring people to himself to share unending life, how can they appreciate what it is they are in danger of losing by their sin?

The compassionate God of Jesus' parables

That is why the constant topic of Jesus' teaching, particularly his parables, is his "Abba." The introductory phrase of each parable, "the kingdom of heaven is like unto. . ." lets us know explicitly that what Jesus is trying to explain is the way in which God works to save humans throughout history. And the range of metaphorical comparisons in the parables tells us how Jesus himself viewed the action of his "Abba." Many of the parables talk about nurturing life—sowing seed in the ground, taking care of the grape vines, watching over the lambs of the flock. Others talk about God *gathering*—crops, or fish, or sheep. Still others have "the king," that is, God, passing judgment—but lenient and forgiving judgment. Perhaps most revealing, a number of parables describe "the king" or the father of a family giving a party, inviting guests to a feast, arranging a celebration. And at least in the case of the parable about the father of the wayward son, the big celebration is being prepared for a sinner who returned. In a number of the parables, the sinner is not described as one who is evil but as one who is "lost"—and when that person is found, "there is rejoicing in heaven."

For his closer friends, Jesus' dearest wish is that they, too, come to know and possess his Father—"I pray that where I am, these also may be." We can imagine the profound joy experienced by the earliest Christians when, after his resurrection, they remembered such sayings of Jesus. Nothing was clearer from his teaching than the fact that God does not wish humans to remain alienated from divine help and forgiveness. As a matter of fact, "God so loved the world that he sent his own only-begotten son, so that those who believe in him may not perish but may have unending life" (John 3:15).

Condemnation of sin

Another feature of Jesus' attitude towards sin and sinners stands in apparent tension with the compassion we have just been describing. Jesus clearly denounces sin and castigates those who will not face up to their sin; and he is particularly hard on those who exploit the weak in society. The scene of his driving the money-changers from the temple courts is a dramatic instance of this.

Really, though, when we reflect on it, we realize that such straightforward confrontation with evil is necessary. It is part of Jesus' desire to reconcile people with themselves and with one another. Jesus "told it as it was," because any genuine reconciliation must be based on truth. Besides, at times it was quite clear that such a strong approach was the only thing that might shake the sinners in question from their complacent sinning.

There is much to be learned from this. We have such a developed capacity to gloss over our sinful actions, to pretend that some particular act is permissible and justified when we know down deep that it is wrong. Or more often, we subtly turn our attention away from the sinfulness of our behavior, not permitting ourselves to slow down and look carefully at what it is that we are doing to ourselves or others.

We do this also in our social behavior, when as groups we pretend that things are other than they truly are. One could point to any number of instances today where we "sweep things under the rug." While a sizable portion of our citizens in this affluent country are on or below the poverty level, we are squandering billions of dollars on useless—even militarily useless!—weaponry. We are still depriving marginated groups— women, Spanish-speaking, blacks, the elderly, among others—of equal opportunity to develop their human potential, to express the native creativity they possess; and hiding behind pat phrases such as "reverse discrimination." We will not listen to the clear evidence that our increasingly comfortable life styles are enjoyed at the price of millions of people starving in the Third World.

Often this unwillingness to face the real evils or problems with which we have to deal can lead to tragic results. How often in a family is the alcoholism, or drug addiction, or sexual abuse of some family member "overlooked" until it is too late? Only very recently, for example, has the whole problem of child sexual abuse come to open public attention. The problem is not new, as many of the stories of adults who were victims of this in their childhood attest, but for generations we hid our heads in the sand, not admitting that the problem existed. This made serious confrontation of the problem impossible.

All of us know that in our life circumstances there are issues that no one wishes to face, conflicts that we gloss over because we are afraid that things will only get worse if we try to resolve the situation, people being hurt because it would be too painful (we think) to open up for candid discussion a problem area that should be handled. And we tell ourselves that we are faith communities, or friendly neighborhoods, or happy families, when in some instances the peace and unity are only skin-deep.

A television program that aired a few years ago illustrated this rather strikingly. It dealt with a Christian congregation in California shortly after the Carter Administration had granted amnesty to young men who had refused military service in the Vietnam War. Surmising that parishioners held very different views on the appropriateness of such amnesty and that this divided opinion reflected long-festering resentments regarding the war itself, the pastor suggested in his sermon that parishioners during the regular Sunday morning coffee hour take up a discussion of the amnesty.

Quite literally, "all hell broke loose." The parish split right down the middle; families that lived next door to one another in apparent friendship now aired their accusatory opinions of one another. One family admitted that they always saw the boy from next door who had gone to Canada to avoid the draft as an irresponsible coward, whereas another family looked on the two young men next door who had eagerly volunteered for military service as naive adventurers. People began to realize that although they appeared to be quite tolerant of opposing views about the legitimacy of the Vietnam War, such was not really the case. Despite their pretense, parishioners on each side judged their "friends" who held an opposite view as either deluded or unpatriotic or selfish or criminally irresponsible.

Painful as the opening of this festering division was, it made it possible for the congregation gradually to come to terms with the resentments under the surface; and slowly a unity grounded in genuine tolerance emerged. This new reconciliation had become possible only because the pastor had not allowed his people to live with the illusion that they were a true community. True peace and unity, genuine reconciliation, in any group must be grounded in truth and justice.

One finds the same kind of behavior in Jesus' dealings with the social divisions of his day. These divisions were very deep, as the tragic history of the ensuing forty years made clear. But when Jesus attempted to draw to the attention of Jewish religious leadership their religious oppression of the common people, the reaction was to accuse Jesus of being an agitator, an accusation they then brought to his trial before Pontius Pilate.

To some extent the accusation was well-grounded; anyone who speaks out on social injustice will disturb people. That Jesus disturbed people seems rather clear—how could it be otherwise for one whose basic role was that of prophet? What is less clear perhaps, though it should not be, is that his disturbing a superficial situation of public order was in itself an essential step in bringing into existence a genuine reconciliation of warring social factions.

There is another important lesson to be gained from the manner in which Jesus dealt with the social alienations and sinful oppressions of his day: in working for justice and peace among his people, Jesus did not ally himself with any of the power blocs of the time. If nothing else makes clear his freedom from partisan loyalties, the fact that he incurred the animosity of each of the opposing factions indicates that he did not commit himself to any political group. Despite their long-standing and deep rivalry, the Pharisees and Sadduccees apparently formed a strange alliance in opposing and then destroying Jesus.

Actually, the social and religious views of Jesus were a challenge to the opposing parties, because his view of God and of Israel transcended theirs. Had they accepted his teaching about the reality of the God of Israel, whom Jesus knew as his "Abba," it would have bypassed and made obsolete the disputes in which they were engaged. More radically, the view of God that he was publicly teaching passed unequivocal judgment upon the kind of power that they were claiming for themselves as Judaism's teachers and leaders. Jesus repudiated that power because it was a major source of alienation, that is, of sinful division, among the people.

According to the gospel of Matthew, the third of the temptations proposed to Jesus in the desert was that of power and wealth. Satan offers to him as the way of accomplishing his messianic missions "all the kingdoms of the earth." Jesus rejected this proffered key to "salvation," and his rejection seems to square with the lesson of history. Without adopting any Marxist theory of class conflict, or any confrontation explanation of social development, it seems rather evident that the divisions between the rich and the poor, between those in power and the powerless, between "important" and "ordinary" people, have always been sources of hostility and alienation.

One has to be very careful in speaking this way, for in themselves wealth and power are not evil. They can be, and sometimes are, the means of bettering the human situation. It would be irresponsibly naive—not to mention ineffective—to work for justice and peace, for reconciliation among people, without dealing honestly and creatively with social power. And much of the power in society comes from wealth.

Wealth and power by themselves, however, do not provide an answer to reconciliation; more often they create the division that must be healed. They tend to build a wall of separation. Jesus, as Ephesians 2:14 tells us, broke down the wall of separation, so that there could be one people. People are united with one another, become a human community, through love and concern for one another. Establishing such a new unified people is meant to begin with the church; it should be a community in which the old discriminations between powerful and powerless no longer have a place, a community which can then work sacramentally to bring reconciliation and peace to the entire human family.

Jesus' teaching and behavior, then, set the pattern for the reconciliation that should mark the life of Christians. But there is a deeper level to Jesus' forgiving and reconciling actions, a level at which we have only hinted. That deeper level is indicated by the word "sacramental"—Jesus' reconciling activity was sacramental of his Father's forgiveness.

When we say this, we are, obviously, pointing to the fact that we can argue from Jesus' forgiveness to the reality of divine forgiveness. Jesus, knowing in unique fashion what it was that God wanted done, dealt with sinners in an understanding and receptive way—so it must be that God wants sinners to be reconciled. Jesus, as John's gospel tells us, was sent by his Father precisely to free humans from evil and to make possible their ultimate possession of unending life—so he told people that this was the source of his forgiving mission. In his unparalleled understanding of his "Abba" Jesus knew, and communicated to people by his teaching, that to be forgiving is the very nature of God.

But "sacramental" carries us further than this. It means that God's forgiving love was present in Jesus' forgiveness of people. Just as my intention to communicate with you and the idea I wish to share are contained in the meaning of the words I speak to you, and the words therefore make me a present to you, so also is the saving God present in the teaching and healing carried on by Jesus. Jesus' forgiveness was not the sign of a distant forgiving God; it was the sacrament of a God who was healing people precisely by presence to them. In experiencing my words you experience me. In experiencing Jesus' forgiveness people were experiencing God's incarnated Word and therefore experiencing God.

Jesus was, and still as the risen Lord is, the sacrament of divine forgiveness. However, because in resurrection he has passed beyond our space and time, he can function now as sacrament only through the agency of the church, which is his body. So, to carry further our understanding of how God's reconciliation with humans takes place, we must turn our attention to reconciliation as it takes place sacramentally in the life of the Christian community.

If anyone among you is suffering hardship, he must pray. If a person is in good spirits, he should sing a hymn of praise. Is there anyone sick among you? He should ask for the presbyters of the church. They in turn are to pray over him, anointing him with oil in the Name [of the Lord]. This prayer uttered in faith will reclaim the one who is ill, and the Lord will restore him to health. If he has committed any sins, forgiveness will be his. Hence, declare your sins to one another, and pray for one another, that you may find healing.

James 5:13-16

CHAPTER SEVEN

Liturgies
of Reconciliation

Working to realize the dream of the church being a community of persons that exists in peace is an unending and immense task. Many things will have to be done, but appropriate liturgies of reconciliation will have to play a key role. Only when we Christians gather together, realizing the saving presence in our midst of the risen Lord and realizing the demands for reconciliation that he lays upon us, will we have the power to overcome the sin in our midst.

It would be a mistake to limit the notion of sacrament to those ritual actions we have called "the seven sacraments." Beyond those rituals lie the broader realities of Christian life—birth and death, developing into maturity, friendship and marriage, working to spread the kingdom—which are truly effective symbols of Christ's death and resurrection, that is, Christian sacraments. However, our sacramental rituals are meant to serve as guides in discovering the deeper meaning of these broader sacramental areas of experience. For this reason, a closer look at the liturgical celebrations of reconciliation may prepare us to understand more accurately the reconciliation that should mark the whole of our Christian lives.

One of the most evident and significant changes in Catholic practice during the past couple of decades has been the shift in the liturgy of reconciliation. Not too long ago, "going to confession" on a weekly or at least frequent basis was a taken-for-granted element in a sincere Catholic's life. Now, for reasons that are not too clear, participation in reconciliation liturgy has declined sharply; for many actively involved and deeply believing people it has simply dropped out of their lives without much notice.

Aware of the need to meet this situation, the Vatican issued a few years ago a revised ritual for the sacrament of reconciliation, proposing three different forms that could be appropriately used according to varying situations. This introduced a much needed element of flexibility; it began to shift the emphasis from people concentrating on their sinfulness to people being grateful for the gift of reconciliation; and it started to move the sacrament from a very individualistic practice into a liturgy to be celebrated by communities of Christians. Important as this shift was, it could not by itself solve the more basic need, namely an *understanding* of the role that liturgy should play in fostering genuine reconciliation in the church.

In the course of the past two millennia the church has seen some drastic changes in its ceremonies for reconciliation of sinners. For many centuries, the official liturgy focused on major offenses such as apostasy or blasphemy or adultery, offenses that were already a matter of public knowledge. After years of doing penance commensurate with the offense, the sinner would be readmitted to full sharing in the community's life and worship, and this would be done in a ceremony of reconciliation in which the entire community participated. During the Middle Ages the practice of private confession began to take hold until it became the common pattern of Catholic practice. Apparently, we are in the beginning stages of another change, though it is too early yet to know clearly what will develop.

What is needed, no matter what precise liturgical forms come into being, is a deepened understanding of how liturgical celebrations are to relate to the rest of life and what function they are meant to play in Christians' growth in faith—in this case the function of liturgies of reconciliation and their relation to the various situations of reconciliation about which we spoke in previous chapters. One general remark seems justified by what we have already seen: since there is a wide variety of reconciliations that occur in our experience, there is a need for a number of reconciliation liturgies that can appropriately celebrate and help achieve the different reconciliations.

Individual reconciliation

No doubt, the most frequent occasion for reconciliation will continue to be that which for centuries has been the exclusive situation: the reconciliation/forgiveness of each of us for the sinfulness we have as individuals. While the newly revised ritual provides for three forms of reconciliation liturgy, all three deal with individuals being forgiven for their sins. There is as yet no provision in the official liturgies for the kind of corporate admission of guilt and corporate reconciliation we will discuss a bit later.

So, in our present liturgy of reconciliation, no matter which of the three forms is used, three results are achieved. Named here, a detailed discussion of each result follows: 1) Reconciliation with one another is effected or, if it already exists to some extent, is extended or deepened. 2) We celebrate the fact that God's saving presence to us has made this human reconciliation possible, and we celebrate the fact that this human reconciliation is sacramental of the divine forgiveness. 3) Each of us is being forgiven for our sinfulness, by ourselves, by our Christian brothers and sisters, and by God—in the way we described in an earlier chapter.

1. Liturgy effects reconciliation

In our attempts to give a theological understanding of the priest's absolution of sins in the confessional, we have always been faced with a question—and we have never been able to give a completely satisfactory answer to the question. We have said that a person who commits a grave sin should repent as quickly as he or she can, and if this repentance is sincere and the person turns to God to ask for forgiveness, the person is forgiven and restored to friendship with God. And we have also said that such contrition for one's sins is the appropriate attitude that a person should have in coming to confess sins in the sacrament of reconciliation. However, if the sin has already been forgiven by God, what does the confessor do when he says "I absolve you from your sin."

Part of the answer, we now know, lies in the fact that in sinning we have been unfaithful to our fellow Christians, we have not followed through on the commitment made to them in our baptism and confirmation. We need to be forgiven by them, reconciled to them. This forgiveness is what the priest, representing the Christian community, expresses in his act of confessional absolution; and this act is sacramental of the enduring divine forgiveness.

Reconciliation with others

Reconciliation with the others in our Christian community is, then, expressed and accomplished in the liturgy of reconciliation. But this still does not completely answer the question: this liturgy itself presupposes that we have forgiven one another, that we are reconciled, and have come together to celebrate this. So what does the liturgy add to the already existent reconciliation?

At least part of the enduring question is rooted in the way we think of forgiveness and reconciliation as a once-and-for-all affair—someone has hurt me, they apologize and make amends, I forgive them, and that is that. But the reality is somewhat different. Repentance, conversion, forgiveness—each of these is a process, something that takes place and comes to full expression over a period of time, sometimes over a long period of time. If I have for many years lived out some sinful attitude, such as hatred of a certain group of people, I will not change overnight; it will take a persevering effort over time to keep from lapsing back into my old ways. Or, on the other hand, if someone has hurt me very deeply, it may take a long time before I can completely forgive that person and no longer seek "to get even."

Saying that we are sorry, saying that we do forgive one another, can be an important part of this continuing repentance and reconciliation. A public occasion, a liturgy when we gather together in the remembered presence of God, provides a situation for such effective deepening of reconciliation.

Other public gatherings can achieve part of this need. For example, some cities plagued by racial strife have found that the situation was helped by having prominent citizens representing the contending groups come together and pledge their resolve to work against the prejudice and hatred. But Christian liturgies of reconciliation add something critical: by including a proclamation of the gospel, which they are meant to do, they give both the deeper motivation for repentance and forgiveness and the basis for hoping that true reconciliation can occur.

Role of scripture

Use of scripture texts in reconciliation liturgies is much more than "ritual window-dressing," a bit of preparation for the essential actions of confession and absolution. It provides a God-given insight into the reality of our sin, but also a reassurance of the saving power of Jesus' death and resurrection that can free us from our sin. The insight coming from the liturgical use of these biblical passages is meant to be the source of a growing atmosphere of reconciliation within a community of Christians; the confessing of sin and the commitment to live in peace occur in liturgy as direct response to the word of God. Proclamation of the biblical passage and response to it are themselves part of a deepening reconciliation of the assembled Christians with God. Those gathered for the liturgy are becoming more genuine "hearers of the word."

Obviously, this entails some explanation of the gospel message used in a given liturgy. As the Constitution on the Sacred Liturgy of Vatican II declares, the people assembled for any liturgy must be given the opportunity to understand what is happening so that they can intelligently participate. This is clearly important in liturgies of reconciliation, where the desired objective is a more profound conversion of people in response to the challenge of the gospel.

Such a response takes place within the awareness of each person and it is this inner response rather than any external actions or words that is the heart of conversion and reconciliation. At the same time, some public action by which people state their repentance and their forgiveness of one another crystallizes the inner attitude. And of course, reconciliation with one another demands some words or actions by which we communicate our desire to forgive and be forgiven. Liturgy is meant to provide just such a situation where we can share our awareness of being forgiven sinners.

2. Celebration of our reconciliation

All sacramental liturgies are meant to be truly human celebrations; and this clearly applies to liturgies of reconciliation. In a world dominated by various alienations, threatened by the ultimate alienation of a thermo-nuclear war, reconciliation among Christians is something to rejoice in, something to be celebrated.

Religious liturgies are by no means the only occasion on which we celebrate, because love and understanding and peace characterize our dealings with one another in families or neighborhoods or other groupings. We do this at parties and barbecues and public holidays. Christian liturgies absorb all this human celebration but add to it a realization that the presence in human lives of God's reconciling power is what overcomes the alienations that all too often wall us off from one another.

Though our own efforts must work to bring about conversion and forgiveness, we cannot accomplish this sheerly by human effort. Christian faith tells us that we need to be saved from our sins. It tells us also that such salvation has occurred, above all in the life and death and resurrection of Jesus of Nazareth who is the Christ, that is, the savior of human history. In liturgy a Christian community expresses its gratitude for this salvation; it rejoices and celebrates the hope it has for the ultimate achievement of peace among humans of all nations and social classes and cultures.

It is not enough, however, to talk rhetorically about the celebratory character of our liturgies of reconciliation. They must become such in people's actual experience—which now they often are not. If we Christians gathered together because we wished to celebrate the fact that God's presence works to free us from the evils that would destroy harmony and friendship among us, we would certainly become more conscious of what "salvation" means. We need to find ways by which our liturgies can truly be occasions of celebration.

3. Forgiveness of sin

As individual confession of sins to a priest from the Middle Ages on became the common pattern of the liturgy of reconciliation, the confessor's act of "absolving" the penitent came to be seen as the moment of sins being forgiven. A person's confessing of sin was an obvious precondition for the action of the priest, and some penance was to be performed after a person was absolved from his or her sins, but the priestly pronouncing of forgiveness was singled out, and by itself considered "the sacramental action."

As important an element in the sacramental liturgy as this act of the confessor is, it was a mistake to give it such exclusive attention. As we saw in an earlier chapter, forgiveness of sin is a

much broader reality; and the entire liturgical ceremony of reconciliation enters into this forgiveness of sin. Liturgies should be
planned so that people can become more clearly and honestly
aware of the ways in which they are not yet fully Christian, so
that they decide to live with greater fidelity, and so that they accept with peace of soul their need for help from God and one
another. As this happens in a carefully created liturgy, the personal reality of "the forgiveness of sin" is happening; and the
human reality is itself sacramental of the divine forgiveness that
is present in the liturgical action.

Because his presbyteral ordination has placed him in a
position to speak and act as a representative of the world-wide
church as well as of the local community, the confessor can bring
to the individual penitent in an official way the church's forgiveness. In this way, the particular liturgy reaches out beyond
the local community and serves to link the forgiven Christian to
the rest of the reconciled people of God. Reconciliation liturgies
should be a key contribution toward the achievement of peace
in the world, for the promise they give is that we can trust that
other peoples will forgive us for what we have done to alienate
them.

Liturgies of corporate repentance

There is increasing awareness today of the systemic character
of much of the real sin in today's world. It is true that systems
as such cannot sin; people sin. But much of the exploitation and
damaging of people comes through activities in which large groups
of us are engaged. As individuals, we would not offend other
people, yet we participate in large companies or clubs or nations
that are involved in activities that destroy people. We are members
of some sports club that excludes certain groups from its membership; we vote for city councilors who have run on a platform
of commercial development that will drive the poor from their
present housing; we invest our money in a company whose profit-
ability comes from exploiting cheap labor in some Third World

country. We say that we disagree with the unjust policy, but we are willing to profit from its implementation.

Because human life is becoming more complex, because in knowledge and production and even recreation we are increasingly interdependent, there are more and more things that we do as groups rather than as individuals. Since these corporate actions have a moral dimension, are good or bad, there is corporate as well as individual sin; consequently there must be corporate repentance, corporate conversion, and corporate reconciliation.

Reconciliation within the church

What applies to society as a whole applies in a distinctive way to the Christian community, the church. As the church, we are meant to be the body of the risen Christ; we exist corporately and are meant to act corporately. In the past half century we have become more aware of being a community, an awareness that had been greatly diminished over the previous half millennium as modern Western culture stressed the individual person.

With this deepened sense of community we can once more think of ourselves as being a people of God rather than a religious organization, we can move toward the use of a family model rather than a political model when we think about ourselves as the church. We realize more sharply that each of us comes to Christian faith in a community and is dependent upon that community for the nurturing and support of faith.

As this recovered realization grew, we found that we had to change some of the things we were accustomed to say about the church. Formerly, when we talked about holiness as a "mark" of the church we said that individual Christians were sinful but that the church as such did not sin; but once we regained the insight that we are the church, we had to acknowledge that the church as such does sin. The church has corporate guilt, has need for corporate acknowledgment of that guilt, need for conversion and repentance, need to be forgiven.

If this is true, we need liturgies in which as a community we pray to recognize our sins, pray to discover the ways in which as a group we do not respond honestly to the challenge of the gospel, pray that God's Spirit will work among us to lead us to genuine conversion. We need liturgies that will give us the public occasion for starting our conversion, for committing ourselves to the tasks of group discipleship that we had neglected, for seeking forgiveness from and reconciliation with those whom we had harmed by our shared attitudes and actions.

Alienations to be healed

There are many situations within the church where reconciliation must take place among groups and where, therefore, there is need for liturgies directed to that goal. Parishes often have distinctive problems to solve along this line. In some instances there are old divisions that grew up because of ethnic rivalries that were rooted in waves of new immigrants moving into established neighborhoods. Or there are wounds left from disputes over things like buying a new church organ, or allocating money for fixing the school rather than the church basement, or having a new pastor fail to support some parish organization that was dear to the heart of at least some parishioners. Or there can be more wrenching divisions as neighborhoods change and the fears and worries about the decline of property values and about the safety of people carry over into church life.

Whatever the precise problems, people find themselves alienated from one another, unwilling even to talk to one another—and often for relatively insignificant reasons. To be what they are meant to be, a genuine community of Christians sharing their faith and concern for another, they need to come together in a situation of prayer to face the sinfulness of their divisions, to resolve together to start building bridges instead of walls, and gradually to forgive and be reconciled with one another.

Beyond the needs for reconciliation that are peculiar to this or that parish group, there are the basic areas of division in society that exist also in the lives of Christians—divisions between rich and poor, powerful and powerless, men and women, young and old. The gospel that is preached to Christians demands the abolition of such alienations, above all among Christians themselves. Yet much of the corporate life of the church reinforces rather than challenges such divisions.

To some extent this is a new way of talking about life within the church. We had grown accustomed to hearing about obedience and submission to church authorities. Now, particularly since the Second Vatican Council, emphasis is being laid on equality and freedom and responsibility. People are understandably a bit confused by this shift; and the shift inevitably brings with it some tension and pain. Basically, though, the pain is the pain of healing as we try together to move toward a church in which there are no class discriminations.

Working to realize the dream of the church being a community of persons that exists in peace is an unending and immense task. Many things will have to be done, but appropriate liturgies of reconciliation will have to play a key role. As the New Testament writings insist, the risen Christ is our peace, the cause of our reconciliation with one another. Only when we Christians gather together, realizing the saving presence in our midst of the risen Lord and realizing the demands for reconciliation that he lays upon us, will we have the power to overcome the sin in our midst. Or to put it another way, only if we share in his Spirit can we become a truly Christian community. Such sharing is not confined to our liturgical gatherings, and the task of working toward reconciliation extends to all of our dealings with one another. But there is a great need for some liturgies of reconciliation to deal directly with these broader social divisions that still alienate us from one another.

Ecumenical liturgies of reconciliation

One last remark about liturgies of corporate sin and corporate reconciliation. Concern about the sinful division in our society is not confined to Catholics nor to Christians. For that reason, there should be and probably will be an increased ecumenical character to our efforts toward peace and justice, and quite logically an increase in ecumenical liturgies of reconciliation. At some point, and probably sooner rather than later, we will need to gather with other people of good will to profess our decision to be reconciled with one another and to admit our need for God's saving power to aid us. When that happens, those liturgies themselves will be a powerful agency for overcoming the divisions that still separate us from one another.

Total reconciliation of humans with one another is not, our faith tells us, a goal that will be achieved short of the parousia. When humans live in full peace, this will be the fulfillment of the kingdom of God and history will have achieved its purpose. In the meantime, it is our responsibility as disciples of the Prince of Peace to work unceasingly for this peace and to gather at times to celebrate together our hope that reconciliation rather than alienation will become the pattern of human society.

If you bring your gift to the altar and there recall that your brother has anything against you, leave your gift at the altar, go first to be reconciled with your brother, and then come and offer your gift.

Matthew 5:23-24

CHAPTER EIGHT

Eucharistic Reconciliation

As we become more conscious that our coming together for eucharist is a gathering at the table of the Lord and at his invitation, we are at least implicitly more aware that we must do so as a family able to celebrate its unity and peace.

When the liturgical movement began to gain momentum and some acceptance in the 1950s and 1960s, the focus in the United States was the annual Liturgical Week. If one goes back to examine the proceedings of those weeks and notices the topics discussed and the governing themes chosen for each year, an interesting fact emerges. While in the earlier years there was an almost exclusive attention to strictly liturgical matters, within a short time there was growing mention of the relation of liturgy to social justice.

In emphasizing this link between worship of God and concern for healing the alienations in society, the liturgical movement recovered one of the most basic tenets in the Jewish and Christian traditions, an element that for some time had been neglected.

At least as far back as the great prophets of Israel, one can find biblical statements about the emptiness of religious ritual performed by those who simultaneously exploit the powerless of society. Jesus of Nazareth continued this prophetic tradition and in his teaching stressed care of the poor and disadvantaged as the will of his Father. The last parable of Jesus contained in the gospels describes "the last judgment" when all humans are brought before him for evaluation of their lives; and the basis of judgment is simply that of feeding the hungry and sheltering the homeless.

Earliest Christianity recognized the link between healing the divisions of society and celebrating the "breaking of the bread" (the eucharist). In his first letter to the community at Corinth, written around the year A.D. 55, St. Paul criticizes severely those who would discriminate between poor and well-to-do when the community gathers for its eucharistic liturgy. As he says, this is a sin against the body of Christ—both the eucharistic body and the body that is the church. In the epistle to the Galatians, he states the basic principle that in the body of Christ there is no place for discrimination on the basis of power or wealth or ethnic origin or gender. Reconciliation is to be a characteristic of the Christian community and its eucharistic gatherings are to celebrate and cement their union in Christ.

Meal of reconciliation

The basic structure of the eucharistic liturgy, that of a meal, indicates the role it is meant to play as a celebration of reconciliation. Eating together has always been and still is a familiar way of indicating a union with one another and, if people had previously been at odds, their reconciliation. In the Temple liturgy of the Old Testament period, the central ritual of the "peace offerings" was celebrated as a sacred meal in which Yahweh and his people joined to renew the covenant, a covenant that the people all too often violated. This "peace offering" was a key element in the religious experience of Jesus and his disciples from which early Christianity drew as its own rituals gradually developed.

Out of the meals when Christians quite naturally gathered to be with one another, to recall and celebrate what had happened in Jesus' life and death and resurrection, to praise Jesus' heavenly Father for this great act of salvation, there emerged very quickly the distinctive celebration we know as the Christian eucharist. But as it emerged, the eucharist remained essentially a community meal that ritualized their peace with one another and with God, a meal that gave thanks for the reconciliation achieved in Jesus' death and resurrection.

Even though for many centuries Christians tended to forget the meal character of eucharist, partially because of theological and doctrinal concentration on the eucharist as a sacrifice, the eucharistic action, the Mass, was always in its essence a meal, a sharing of food and drink—bread and wine transformed into Christ's gift of his own life-giving body and blood. In the past half-century, both theologians and liturgical scholars have realized again the central importance of the meal aspect of eucharist; and this realization is beginning to have its effect on our understanding of and participation in the eucharist.

As we become more conscious that our coming together for eucharist is a gathering at the table of the Lord and at his invitation, we are at least implicitly more aware that we must do so as a family able to celebrate its unity and peace. For any Christian group to assemble for eucharist when unresolved major divisions exist in the group is a charade; it pretends to be a celebration and pledge of forgiveness and reconciliation when the people gathered there intend no such thing. Such an eucharist is as inappropriate as would be a Thanksgiving dinner to which family members came, hostile to one another, disliking and even hating one another, and with no intention of trying to make peace and heal the antagonisms that divide them. One would ask such a family why they bother to get together.

Anamnesis of Jesus' reconciliating act

However, the eucharist is more than an acknowledgment of reconciliation among a group of Christians, a celebration of their peace. It is the root source of that peace.

Eucharist plays this key role in bringing about reconciliation, because it is the *anamnesis,* the making present of Jesus' death and resurrection by which the final reconciliation was introduced into our human history. Paul among first-generation Christians lays greatest stress on this peace-making aspect of Jesus' Passover. In several passages he speaks of the way in which Jesus has broken down the walls of separation, has brought those whose sins alienated them from God once more into union with that God.

When we say that eucharist is *anamnesis* of Jesus' death and resurrection, we are trying to say that the eucharist we celebrate is more than a commemoration of Jesus' Passover, that it is more than the occasion on which the power of that saving action touches our lives. Eucharist is the mystery of Christ's presence in our midst. Presence is something that has to do with people being for one another and communicating with one another. What happens in eucharist is that the risen Christ is himself present, sharing himself with his friends, saying to them through the transformed bread and wine that he exists to be the source of their personal life and growth. Eucharist is more than a recollection of Jesus' resurrection; it is that resurrection, for the resurrection is nothing other than the risen Jesus himself.

And because the risen Lord is present among any group of assembled Christians, forgiveness of one another is a characteristic of any group that identifies itself as Christian. Because the Christ in our midst forgives each of us, extends to each of us a love whose fidelity reflects his Father's love for us, no one of us can truly respond to that offer of Christ's friendship while at the same time refusing to be reconciled with anyone else to whom Christ is also bonded in love.

Just as in a family, a child cannot genuinely and fully respond to a parent's love and at the same time remain unforgiving and alienated from a brother or sister. That which is the source of reconciliation in such instances is precisely the love of the parent for both of them. So, the common bond that Christians have to the risen Christ is the ultimate source of the reconciliation and peace that unites people into one family of God. And above all, when Christians gather together in eucharist to share in the one body of Christ and to become thereby that body of Christ which is the church, reconciliation is celebrated and deepened. Needless to say, the extent to which this happens is conditioned by the extent to which those participating in the liturgy are aware that this is occurring—an eucharist routinely performed and empty of meaning will not signify nor achieve the reconciliation that should take place.

In the reconciliations that should take place within the church itself, particularly the reunion of the various Christian denominations, it is important to remember that the only ultimate and adequate source of reconciliation is the risen Christ. Official actions, theological reflection, pastoral exhortation, all have their place; but in the last analysis it will be Christian relationship to Christ, their acceptance of genuine discipleship, that will lead them to a concerned and forgiving acceptance of one another.

Epiklesis, the reconciling Spirit

Essential as is the element of *anamnesis* in Christian eucharist, it must always be accompanied by the transforming power of God that touches both the assembled Christians and the symbolizing elements of bread and wine. So, in all the liturgies of the church, especially in Eastern Christianity, the *epiklesis,* the invocation of God's Spirit, has played a prominent role. In what is really a continuing Pentecost, the eucharist celebrates and deepens the risen Christ's gift of his Spirit to his disciples.

In the invocation of Christ's Spirit that forms an element of the Eucharistic Prayer (formerly the Canon of the Mass), the assembled Christians pray that this Spirit will through the change of bread and wine change themselves into the one body of Christ.

It is, then, the church's most constant and focal prayer for true unity of the people of God. But it is a prayer that recognizes that the desired unity does not yet fully exist; there are still alienations of one sort or another that need to be removed; there is still need for a deeper and more encompassing forgiveness among the people who make up the church; the family of God is not yet as committed to peace, even in its own life, as it should be.

Even psychologically, this eucharistic *epiklesis,* if it becomes a genuine expression of the community's desire for peace and reconciliation, will become a source of such peace. To wish to forgive and be forgiven is already the biggest step towards such forgiveness. To state publicly together that they share this wish, as Christians do in eucharist, creates a basic understanding and attitude that can then lead to more complete reconciliation. Special liturgies or reconciliation, such as those we discussed in the previous chapter, have this same objective; but the eucharist as the *anamnesis* of Easter and Pentecost celebrates and fulfills what those other liturgies begin to achieve.

Eucharistic peace

It is not accidental that the eucharistic prayer is followed by the "Our Father" with its petition "Forgive us our sins as we forgive those who sin against us," and by the sharing of peace among the assembled people. Peace is both the context and the fruit of eucharistic liturgy.

"Peace" when applied to eucharist must be understood against the background of God's centuries-long working in history, first with Israel and then with the Christian church. "Peace" in that context has a rather precise meaning, one that extends far beyond mere absence of conflict. It is a meaning that flows from the reality of *covenant.*

As the traditions of Israel that are distilled into the Bible tell us, Israel existed as God's people because God chose them and formed an alliance, a covenant, with them. It was not only the ordinary forces of social change and economics and political activity that explain their distinctive identity and role in human history; it was the bond established at Sinai that made and makes Israel Israel. For it was at Sinai, during the rooting experience of the exodus from Egypt, that through the mediation of Moses the people accepted the divine election and Yahweh revealed that "You will be my people and I will be your God."

This covenant was, then, the formative bond, the special social contract, that linked the Old Testament people to God and to one another. Not that the people always remained faithful to the pledges of Sinai; more than once they needed prophets to remind them of the covenant, to lead them to conversion and to reconciliation with their God. But to the extent that the covenant was observed, particularly by honoring social justice within the life of the people, peace resulted. Peace, *shalom,* was the situation that existed when the relationships appropriate to the covenant, Israelites to one another and Israelites to Yahweh, were respected. When justice and concern for the poor and weak characterized Israelitic society, when ritual honor of Yahweh was sincere and from the heart, when kings ruled by true law and not by whim, when prophets spoke truth, then there was peace. For it was then that the Spirit of the Lord permeated the life of the people.

In the theology of the New Testament literature, Jesus himself is seen to be the new covenant; instead of a law and a contractual agreement, it is a person who bonds humans and God. And it is when humans accept in faith the self-gift of the risen Christ that friendship between people and their God is created by the sharing of a common Spirit. This is true peace. So, in the gospel narratives about Easter, the risen Jesus is described as coming to his disciples with the greeting, "Peace be to you. Receive the Holy Spirit."

To the extent that Christians are open to this gift of Christ's Spirit, they are open to one another. This Spirit is the personal power of divine love, creative of community that is grounded in love, creative of people as they learn to love maturely. Those who live by this Spirit live in peace, even when the externals of their lives are disturbed by misfortunes and oppression and mis-understanding. They live at peace with themselves and with one another. They are genuinely reconciled to human life as it is, even while they work to change it into the kingdom of God.

Such is the peace that Christians are meant to pledge to one another in eucharistic liturgy when, between the eucharistic prayer and their communing in the body of Christ, they wish one another the peace of Christ. It is one of the blessings of recent enrich-ment of ritual within the church that we are again able in eucharist to express our wish of peace for one another. Like other liturgical revisions, though, the giving of the peace can be relatively routine and perfunctory or it can have the meaning it is intended to have. When it is done carefully and as a natural and sincere human action, it is automatically a gesture of reconciliation. Whatever barriers might separate two people who exchange the eucharistic gesture of peace, the sharing of Christ's peace is an implicit pledge to overcome these barriers. Obviously, this needs to be explained to people so that they will understand what they are doing.

Celebrating one another

When people are genuinely forgiving and reconciled to one another, they are content to deal with each other as they are. They can quite realistically recognize the shortcomings that others, and they themselves, have but at the same time be grateful for those with whom they are sharing life.

There are obvious advantages that come when one is sur-rounded in one's work and neighborhood and public involve-ments with people who are friendly and trustworthy. Beyond that is the benefit that comes when one is part of a genuine community. In such a group of people, one can feel at home, can share in-terests and activities, can find sympathy and support, can in the deepest sense relax and be oneself, can be at peace. Christian com-munities are meant to be such, and their community celebra-tions—the eucharist in particular—should humanly and simply express their gratitude for the Christian sharing they enjoy.

Clearly, if people gathered together are happy to be together, grateful that they share in a true community of friends who care for one another, they are basically reconciled with one another. Their celebration of reconciliation at a liturgy such as the eucharist does not even have to make explicit mention of reconciliation. On most occasions it would be more appropriate simply to realize that they are celebrating one another. The rituals of eucharist would allow them to do what many people find embarrassing to do individually, to say how much they appreciate one another. If this is said, it confirms whatever forgiveness and reconciliation took place in the previous history of the group.

Daily reconciliation

We might mention one last aspect of the eucharist as the most important sacrament of reconciliation. Christian sacramental liturgies are not meant to be isolated religious events; they are somehow meant to deepen the meaning of our entire life. Most of the liturgies of sacraments, however, deal with special moments of Christian experience—being initiated in baptism, formally entering upon a more adult stage of Christian life in confirmation, being empowered for ministry in an ordination ceremony. It is the eucharist that is the liturgy of our day-by-day attempts to live out the Christ mystery.

What should happen in our eucharistic liturgies is that with some regularity, such as each Sunday, the happenings of our lives are brought into contact with the gospel. As eucharist proclaims the gospel, challenges to conversion, and points us in hope towards the final realization of our potential as the individuals we are, the relatively humdrum course of our lives takes on deeper meaning and the responsibilities of our particular situation become less avoidable. At the same time, hearing the gospel in the light of what is actually taking place in our lives makes Christian beliefs come to life; we understand what Christianity is by trying to be Christian.

Since the need for forgiveness and reconciliation is something that runs throughout our daily experience, usually in small ways, the regular celebration of eucharist inevitably deals with this continuing reconciliation. Eucharistic liturgies can do this in very specific ways, treating the particular situation of a given group instead of expressing only a broad and general Christian attitude of forgiveness.

Naturally, for eucharistic liturgies to function in this way, the communities that celebrate eucharist must understand that this is what is meant to occur and plan their liturgical celebrations to achieve this goal. This can happen in different ways— as part of the initial recognition of sinfulness and need for forgiveness, or as an element in the homily, or in conjunction with the prayers of the faithful, or along with the giving of peace, or as part of the explained meaning of receiving communion. What is important is that those creating and those participating in liturgy come to understand the intrinsic nature of Eucharist as a celebration of Christian reconciliation, of Christian peace.

In proportion as Christian celebrations of eucharist do become liturgies of peace and forgiveness, they will act as sacraments, and therefore causes, of the peace which God intends for the entire human family. Then will the kingdom come, then will God's will be done.

All this has been done by God, who has reconciled us to himself through Christ and has given us the ministry of reconciliation. I mean that God, in Christ, was reconciling the world to himself, not counting men's transgressions against them, and that he has entrusted the message of reconciliation to us. This makes us ambassadors for Christ, God as it were appealing through us. We implore you, in Christ's name: be reconciled to God! For our sakes God made him who did not know sin, to be sin, so that in him we might become the very holiness of God.

2 Corinthians 5:18-21

CHAPTER NINE

Christian Reconciliation

People and their actions are sacramental to the extent that they are significant, that they have a meaning beyond just their external, immediately observable, appearance. They are religiously sacramental if this deeper meaning has to do with the saving presence of God. People and their actions have Christian sacramentality if they signify the presence of the risen Christ working with his Father and their Spirit to transform history.

Liturgies of reconciliation and the eucharist in particular leave no room for doubt: Christian communities should be characterized by a spirit of genuine reconciliation. Yet, as long as history continues, the need to heal alienations in the church and beyond that to heal the alienations in human society will remain a ministerial imperative. In a sense, the whole of Christian ministry is directed to this goal. Because the task is so all-encompassing, this present chapter will suggest only a few instances of reconciliation within the church itself that are especially critical at this point in history. Were healing to occur in the four areas which we will study, it would transform the life of the church.

The pages of the New Testament make clear how deep was Jesus' desire that his followers remain reconciled with one another, despite the occasional differences that occur in any group of people. John's gospel, in particular the discourse of Jesus at the Last Supper, conveys this desire. "I pray, Father, that [the disciples] may be one. . . . By this shall everyone know that you are my disciples, that you have love one for another."

The essence of personal unity among any group of people is mutual love. But because we humans almost inevitably hurt one another, even when we are close friends, love must often be expressed in forgiveness and reconciliation. It is part of maturity to recognize that we are never totally faithful to the friends we cherish, to admit to ourselves and to our friends this limitation, and to be understanding and accepting of the "offenses" of others against us.

A few years ago the movie *Love Story* contained the lines, "Loving means never having to say 'I'm sorry.'" Now that may or may not be a good line in the sentimental context of the movie, but the statement is not true of real life situations. In our real dealings with one another as friends, it is important that we recognize the times that we hurt those we love and that we tell one another that we are sorry, that we need to be forgiven, that we wish to be reconciled.

The phrase of the Our Father is much more realistic: "Forgive us our sins as we forgive those who sin against us." Not only do those words recognize our constant need to be reconciled with God and with one another, they propose the kind of forgiveness we hope for from God as a model for the manner in which we should be forgiving of one another. We have already described the teaching of Jesus about his "Abba's" unqualified forgiveness of us humans; and while we are incapable of being as totally compassionate and magnanimous as God is, we are meant as Christians to strive for this attitude toward our fellow humans.

If Christians were to live compassionately, honestly recognizing their common human need to be forgiven now and then by one another, working to achieve reconciliation rather than nurturing the jealousies and resentments and hostilities that alienate people from each other, this would be a major contribution to a better world. Their behavior toward one another would be proof that humans can live in peace, and so would be a living source of hope to so many others who despair of the human race ever living free of conflict and hatreds and war.

Having said that, we need to deepen our understanding of the effects of Christian reconciliation. Just as we saw that Jesus' forgiving behavior had a more profound, sacramental, level because it flowed from God's forgiveness, expressed that forgiveness and actually made God present to people in an act of forgiveness, so, too, is Christian reconciliation a sacrament. It is a sign that points to the God worshipped by Christians as a forgiving God; but beyond that it actually makes God's forgiving present and active in people's lives.

What that means is that the power working in Christian lives, indeed in the lives of all those who live honestly and with concern for one another, is God's own power to reconcile—ultimately this is the infinite power of divine love that is God's own Spirit. Christians possess this power to transform human history, to change it from the sad tale of wars upon wars upon wars, not because they of themselves are better people, but because they are the body of the risen Christ.

The church, sacrament of reconciliation

As the body of Christ, the Christian community makes the risen Lord present to people, allows him to continue his ministry of reconciliation in history. But this happens only in so far as Christians are a community of people marked by their forgiveness of one another and their active desire to achieve reconciliation in the entire human family. Christian reconciling activity is God's reconciling activity—not in the sense that what we do substitutes now for what God would do, nor in the sense that God approves of what we do and ratifies it as his own, but in the sense that there is a genuine co-doing in which God's forgiving works in and through our forgiving and makes ours possible and effective.

This sacramental character of the church is something to which the Second Vatican Council drew people's attention. The problem is that having once more spoken of the church in this way we will add "sacrament" to the list of other words we use about the church without particularly paying attention to their implications. In the case of "sacrament" there is a special need to probe its meaning and to put it into practice, because the sacramentality of the church exists only in so far as Christians, individually and as a community, actually signify Christ to the world.

People and their actions are sacramental to the extent that they are significant, that they have a meaning beyond just their external, immediately observable, appearance. They are religiously sacramental if this deeper meaning has to do with the saving presence of God. People and their actions have Christian sacramentality if they signify the presence of the risen Christ working with his Father and their Spirit to transform history.

So, the reconciliation that exists among Christians, their recognition of the need to be forgiven by one another and their mature and gracious willingness to forgive others, is a sign of the presence of the risen reconciling Lord among them. This reconciliation works as a sign most directly upon Christians themselves; their own experience of being part of such a forgiving group of people makes credible the forgiving reality of God. But this awareness is more than theoretical; being exposed to others' forgiveness inclines any Christian to be forgiving. The reconciliation that exists in the church is not only significant, it is effective; it helps bring about continuing forgiveness.

Obviously, though, we are far from being completely reconciled to one another in the church. Despite the basic unity and peace for which we are grateful, there are still many divisions that need to be healed. To quite an extent full reconciliation is a goal we need to achieve; the measure of its achievement will be the measure of our sacramental effectiveness in today's world. It will be hypocritical of us to lament the lack of peace in the world, to criticize those whose greed and lust for power divide our world into hostile groups if we do not have our own house in order. So, with love but also with honesty we must face the alienations and conflicts that exist in the church, discover and admit them and then work together to heal them.

There are four basic divisions to which we might point as reconciling tasks we need to address—the incomplete ecumenical reunion of the Christian churches, the split between so-called "progressives" and "reactionaries," the socioeconomic gap between rich/powerful and poor/powerless, and the unequal status and role of women and men in the church. To some extent, each of these is at present a scandal in the technical sense, that is, a barrier to people seeing the church as a manifestation of God's saving action in Christ.

Ecumenical reunion

One of the most exciting and encouraging aspects of twentieth-century Christianity has been the effort of the Christian churches to heal the split that has divided East from West for a millennium and the fragmentation of Western Christianity that occurred in the sixteenth century. Particularly since the formation of the World Council of Churches in 1948 there has been a systematic effort among Protestants and Orthodox to bring about a reunion. While at the beginning there was no Roman Catholic participation, this has gradually changed, with Catholics being present as invited observers at the periodic international meetings of the World Council and Protestant and Orthodox theologians being officially invited observers at Vatican II.

There has been a continuing study of doctrinal "problems" that are possible barriers to full unity. This has produced research reports indicating that for the most part no irreconcilable barriers exist. On the local level there has been a considerable increase in cooperation of various kinds among Catholics and Protestants and Orthodox, along with a reaching out to other religious communities like the Jewish or Islamic or Buddhist. One can safely say that there has been a notable lessening of the bitterness and hostility that formerly marked the relationship between Catholics and Protestants and between East and West.

Yet, much remains to be accomplished. Considerable good will still exists, but the wind seems to have gone out of the sails. The enthusiasm that came, particularly with Vatican II and its Decree on Ecumenism, has given way to relative disinterest on the part of most people. Those professionally involved with ecumenical activities have, fortunately, remained creative and involved; but for most other people, many of whom were earlier quite alert to and excited about possibilities of reunion, the issue of ecumenism has been "put on the back burner." There is real danger that we will drift back into the attitude of taking the division of Christianity for granted.

Because Christianity is what it is, reunion cannot be simply a question of the various churches being willing to recognize the good will and positive value of one another. It must go beyond a decision to keep on co-existing with increased respect and even concern for one another. Accepting the value of legitimate pluralism of understanding and practices, the church is meant to be one community. This community is not primarily one of external organization or institutional structures, but one of shared faith and hope in the risen Christ and of love for one another in the one Spirit.

For such community to exist, a genuine reconciliation must take place. As individuals and particularly as churches, we must express our repentance for previous prejudice and hostility, for the hurt we caused one another, for the arrogance with which we passed judgment upon one another's views and practices. More importantly, we must convert to an attitude of listening and learning from one another, sharing differing insights rather than debating to discredit the other. This shift in attitude toward one another whereby we really begin to develop a shared identity as *Christian* must take place on the official level and it must take place on the grass roots level in the lives of the people who make up the various churches.

"Progressives" and "reactionaries"

Before we even begin to discuss this point, it is important to note the radical inadequacy of designations such as "progressive," "reactionary," "radical," "left wing," "right wing." For the most part they tend to be used to characterize someone else; most of us tend to think of ourselves as quite sensibly moderate and "in the middle." Even more misleading is the use of "liberal" or "conservative." However, there is an undeniable and growing polarizing of attitudes and values in the United States and a comparable polarizing in the Christian churches.

Given the increasing complexity and rapid change of life today, this polarizing is not surprising. And when one considers the radical nature of the shifts occurring in Christianity, it would be most surprising if there were not some such gap between those who wish to stress continuity with the past and those who wish to stress discontinuity and create a distinctively new future. But the problem is that the present tension involves pain, for some people a great deal of pain—and much of the pain comes because people feel themselves often alienated from and in conflict with the very persons who should be their closest allies.

For Catholics—and to some extent for others as well— Vatican II opened up new vistas: the church exists to create a new world, a more truly human history; it opened up new roles for the laity, who are to minister as well as be ministered to. It suggested a new identity to be shared by clergy and laity alike: together and in equality they form the one community of believers, one people of God. For some, all this has proved exciting and hope-filled; but for others it has been a source of fear and dismay. And because the eager expectancy was probably a bit naive, underestimating the immensity of the changes that had begun; and on the other side the worries that made change look more threaening to "tradition" then it actually is, and preserving tradition more of an unqualified imperative than it truly is, there has been a backlash that is quite understandable.

Many people, some of them at the highest levels of the church, who did not wish for a Second Vatican Council in the first place and who tried to keep it from the innovative positions it eventually took, are trying to reverse the direction initiated by the Council. Naturally this distresses those for whom the Council was a genuine awakening of their faith and a new commitment to discipleship and who now feel frustrated and betrayed by former friends or church officials who work against them. In some situations this has led to a dangerous division among Catholics, one that needs to be healed quickly before it eventuates into open rupture.

What is needed is not further accusations, more recrimination, a hardening of positions; what is called for is unprejudiced trust in each other's sincerity, so that there can be a mature sharing of worries and convictions and insights and faith. Reconciliation will not happen of itself; people in each camp must fearlessly and honestly undertake the task of listening and responding that can lead to deepened understanding and eventual appreciation of views that now appear unacceptable. Working for reconciliation between these opposing parties in the church is one of the most challenging and needed ministries in the church today.

Powerful and powerless

The third situation in which considerable division exists in the church comes from conditions in society as a whole, namely the gap between rich and poor, between those who wield power and those who are powerless to control even their own lives. Such a gap has existed as far back as we can trace history; the Bible itself refers to it as something unacceptable to God. However, the problem has taken on a new dimension in recent centuries, which means that the solution toward which Christians must contribute is also somewhat new.

What is increasingly the case today is that the line is drawn between rich nations and poor nations, not just between poor and rich individuals. The rich and the powerful today are groups of people banded together to control the activities of millions of others; they are corporations whose size and outreach is sometimes greater than that of smaller countries.

Most of the earth's millions belong to the poorer nations. We refer to them as the Third World, not because they are an organized bloc that can offset the interlocking power of the United States, Europe, and Japan, but because together they share the fate of being underdeveloped and struggling to keep their people from starvation. They are the countries presently struggling to pay back debts made almost impossible because of unjustly high interest rates imposed by banks in "the first world." Governments in many of these countries are faced with the impossible dilemma: take care of their people and forget about paying back all the debt—in which case they risk losing the capital they need to develop their economy, or impose inhumanly stringent economic measures on their people—in which case violent overthrow of the government is almost guaranteed.

Clearly, this worldwide division among nations is one of explosive alienation. Already the world is filled with constant flare-ups of revolution and counter-revolution. Terrorism threatens even the most powerful of countries. The United States, for example, is every day faced with danger to its embassies abroad. American business people working in foreign countries are being trained in ways of avoiding kidnapping or assassination; and in self-defense or retaliation the United States finds itself employing forms of terrorism that are incompatible with the moral principles that we claim to espouse.

One could go on, painting a rather bleak picture of the conflict between the economically and militarily strong nations and the weaker peoples who are finding new sources of power with which to challenge their stronger opponents. What is more important, though, is to talk about the ways in which this dangerous situation can be changed, how some steps toward reconciliation can be initiated.

Responsibility for such a change rests very heavily on Christians. In many of the powerful countries that could, if they so wished, take the initiative in reversing present inequities, the majority of people are Christian—or at least profess to be. They have the practical possibility of working toward international reconciliation, or for that matter of working toward reconciliation between rich and poor in their own countries. On the other hand, in many of the poorer nations the church would be—and fortunately in some instances is becoming—an influential voice in advocating economic and political measures that foster the well-being of all the people and lead towards a reconciliation of the various sectors of society.

Perhaps even more important: in its membership the church bridges the gap between "the worlds." Not only is it long established as the primary religious faith in many of the rich nations, it is the basic religio-cultural context of life in large areas of deprivation such as Central and Latin America and is expanding rapidly in Africa. In theory, at least, a large portion of both sectors, rich and poor, should regard one another as fellow believers, as brothers and sisters. If it were truly one community in faith and mutual concern, Christianity would be a potent force for reconciliation and peace in the world.

The gospel imperative to realize this potential is unmistakable. Continuing the Israelitic prophets' emphasis on God's concern for the poor, Christianity from its earliest days insisted on what today is being called "the preferential option for the poor." As Jesus' own ministry testified, there is divine concern for all people, rich as well as poor—Jesus preached to both and healed both. Yet, Jesus clearly paid greater attention to those in society who were less able to protect and care for themselves. And Paul, in his letter to the Galatians (3:28), stated the basic principle that in the body of Christ which is the church there is to be no discrimination, economic, social, or sexual, between the powerful and the powerless.

Early Christianity spoke of Jesus as having come to break down the walls that separated people from one another (Ephesians 2:14). In today's world the continuation of this ministry of breaking down walls needs to be seen in terms of the worldwide forces that are building such walls. Genuine reconciliation can take place only if the basic causes of alienation are eliminated. This does not mean that Christians should oppose technological or organizational progress; it does mean that such progress should not be gained at the price of people.

Sexism in the church

The fourth and final instance of reconciliation we will examine here, the need for reconciliation between women and men in the church, is closely related to what we have just been discussing. Women are disproportionately represented among the world's poor and powerless.

The church should be in the forefront of the movement to reverse the centuries-long discrimination against women. Yet, traditionally in the church neither the status nor the role of women is equal to that of men, even in those Christian denominations that admit women to ordination. In the Catholic church there is, of course, the denial to women of full ministerial opportunity. But more than that, official statements have attempted to justify this limitation of women by saying that it is rooted in divine revelation,—which would imply that not only church officials but God also is downgrading women.

It would be both inaccurate and unjust, however, to put all the blame on officialdom in the church. The problem goes much deeper. Christianity, emerging and developing as it did in the context of patriarchal culture, absorbed the presuppositions and prejudices of that culture regarding male superiority. Even when it did not formally teach the inferiority of women, it built that judgment into its structures and its symbolism. And the increased clericalism of the church fed into and intensified this denigration of women.

Today we are beginning to know better. As society in general is growing in awareness of the alienation between women and men that is grounded in male domination of women, the church, too, is discovering its sin in this regard. But even as the abstract understanding gains some acceptance, the practical implementation moves very slowly. For a variety of reasons, both women and men hesitate to realign the structures and functions and responsibilities of church life in a way that grants opportunity on the basis of personal competence regardless of gender. And for the moment at least, Christians are not exerting obvious leadership in overcoming this long-standing alienation.

Basically, the reconciliation between men and women in the church will have to consist in a fundamental change of attitude, for both women and men have inherited the discriminatory outlook of their culture. Christians will need to become a strong counter-cultural force, something that they have not thought of themselves as being for a long time. As women begin to occupy positions of equality, it will be a new and for some people an unsettling experience; it will be truly a sacrament of the divine saving power working independently of sexual identity.

After centuries of this unquestioned discrimination, reconciliation will not come easily or quickly. There will have to be a dedicated, patient ministry to reconciliation, one that takes account of and works to overcome resentments and prejudices and fears. For a Christian conscience, however, there is no alternative. Having once discovered, as we now have, that sexism is a sin that needs to be eradicated from society and even more so from the Christian community, we must go on to repent of it and be converted to true Christian egalitarianism.

These four areas of needed reconciliation within the church are not the only ones that need attention; we could have pointed to the racial prejudices that still afflict Christian communities, or to the generational conflicts, or to tensions between ethnic groups. However, these four illustrate the fact that there still exists a massive task of reconciliation within the church before it can become as sacramentally effective in the world as it is intended by God to be.

Complete peace among humans is not something to be anticipated before the achievement of the kingdom of God at the end of history. Certain conflicts of interest appear inevitable and will need to be resolved by mature negotiation. But the alienations that come from greed and exploitation and hatred, that is, those that are rooted in sin and that are intrinsically destructive of people, can be overcome. To believe that and to do something about it is at the very heart of Christianity.